TOP NOTCH FUNDAMENTALS

Workbook

Joan Saslow ■ Allen Ascher

with Julie C. Rouse

PEARSON
Longman

Top Notch: English for Today's World   FUNDAMENTALS
Workbook

Pearson Education, 10 Bank Street, White Plains, NY 10606

Editorial director: Pamela Fishman
Senior development editor: Marcia Schonzeit
Assistant editor: Siobhan Sullivan
Vice president, director of design and production: Rhea Banker
Director of electronic production: Aliza Greenblatt
Managing editor: Mike Kemper
Senior production editor: Sasha Kintzler
Art director: Ann France
Senior manufacturing buyer: Dave Dickey
Photo research: Aerin Csigay
Text composition: Word & Image Design Studio, Inc.
Full-service production provided by Camelot Editorial Services
Text font: Frutiger 10/12
Cover Photograph: "From Above," by Rhea Banker. Copyright © 2005 Rhea Banker.

ISBN: 0-13-110661-9

Photo credits:

Page 1 (1) Cat Gwynn/Getty Images, (2) Thierry
Roge/Reuters/Corbis, (3) Carlos Alvarez/Getty Images,
(4) Susana Gonzalez/Getty Images; p. 2 (top) Robert
Mora/Getty Images, (bottom) Sonora, Inc.; p. 4 (left) Steve
Finn/Getty Images, (right) Frank Micelotta/Getty Images;
p. 5 (left) Alan Bolesta/Index Stock I8magery, (middle) Getty
Images, (right) Getty Images; p. 13 (top) Bill Aron/
PhotoEdit, (bottom) Jeff Greenberg/PhotoEdit; p. 14 (left)
Michael Newman/PhotoEdit, (middle) John Elk III, (right)
Steven Dunwell/Getty Images; p. 16 (1) Leisa Johnson/
Index Stock Imagery, (2) Paul Katz/Index Stock Imagery,
(3) Henryk T. Kaiser / Index Stock Imagery, (4) Gary Conner/
Index Stock Imagery, (5) Thomas A. Kelly/Corbis, (6) Alan
Schein Photography/Corbis; p. 19 (1) Tim Graham/Corbis, (2)
Corbis, (3) Pierre-Philippe Marcou/AFP/Getty Images,
(4) Tim Graham/Corbis, (5) Tim Graham/Corbis; p. 27 Azzara
Steve/Corbis Sygma; p. 44 (top) Reuters/Corbis, (bottom left)
Bettmann/Corbis, (bottom right) Miramax/Dimension Films
/ The Kobal Collection / Sorel, Peter; p. 46 (left) Tom & Dee
Ann McCarthy/Corbis, (middle) Getty Images, (right)
Royalty-Free/Corbis; p. 62 Comstock Images; p. 67 (left inset)
Original Films/The Kobal Collection, (left) Graham
French/Masterfile, (right) AFP/Corbis; p. 68 Alison
Wright/Corbis; p. 73 Doug Pensinger/Getty Images;
p. 82 (left) Bettmann/Corbis, (right) AP Photo/Alberto
Pellaschiar.

Illustration credits:

Steve Attoe: pages 2, 28 (top), 80; Kenneth Batelman:
page 17; Leanne Franson: pages 3, 7, 20, 25, 49; Scott
Fray: page 59; Brian Hughes: page 84; Steve Hutchings:
pages 37, 55, 62; Suzanne Mogensen: pages 1, 21, 26,
59, 79; Dusan Petriçic: pages 47, 53 (top), 54 (bottom),
67, 87 (center, right); Michelle Rabagliati: pages 31, 33
(top); Phil Scheuer: pages 53 (bottom), 54 (top), 73, 77,
85, 86, 87 (left); Steve Schulman: pages 32, 33 (bottom),
41; Jessica Miller-Smith: page 71; Neil Stewart: pages
13, 15, 18, 28 (bottom), 40, 48; Anna Veltfort: pages 8,
53 (bottom), 66, 77.

Printed in the United States of America
11 12 13 14 15 16–VHG–12 11 10 09 08

CONTENTS

UNIT 1

Names and Occupations

LESSON 1

 Look at the pictures. Write occupations for the places.

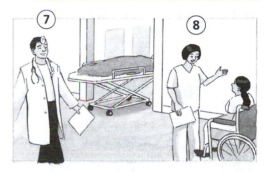

1. _a teacher_
2. _____

3. _____
4. _____

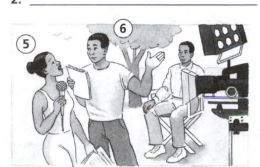

5. _____
6. _____

7. _____
8. _____

 FAMOUS PEOPLE. What are their occupations? Write sentences. Use contractions.

1. Frank Gehry: _He's an architect_____.

2. Lance Armstrong: _____.

3. Shakira: _____.

4. Denzel Washington: _____.

1

3 Complete the conversation between Denzel Washington and Nora.

1. **Denzel Washington:** Hi, I'm Denzel.

   Nora: Hi, _____ .

2. **Denzel Washington:** Nice to meet you, Nora.

   Nora: _____ .

3. **Denzel Washington:** What do you do?

   Nora: _____ .

   _____ ?

   Denzel Washington: I'm an actor.

LESSON 2

4 Circle the occupation that is different.

1. scientist	doctor	(chef)	nurse
2. teacher	actor	singer	musician
3. artist	pilot	architect	photographer
4. lawyer	manager	athlete	banker

5 Look at the people going to work. Write sentences about their occupations. Use contractions.

1. *She's an artist* _____ .

2. _____ .

3. _____ .

4. _____ .

5. _____ .

6. _____ .

Complete the sentences with names.

1. My favorite singer is _____.
2. My favorite actor is _____.
3. My favorite athlete is _____.
4. My favorite artist is _____.
5. _____ is a famous musician.
6. _____ is a famous writer.

 Read the list. Then look at the pictures and complete the conversations.

Name	Occupation
Anna Madden	Pilot
Maggie Gill	Singer
Julia Santos	Nurse
Grace Lund	Scientist
Emily Parson	Student
Caroline Benson	Lawyer
Nicole Locke	Student

Are you Maggie?

1. _No, I'm not._
I'm Grace.

Are you Anna?

2. _____
_____

Are you Caroline?

3. _____
_____

Are you Emily and Nicole?

4. _____
_____

8 ▷ **Read about Madonna.**

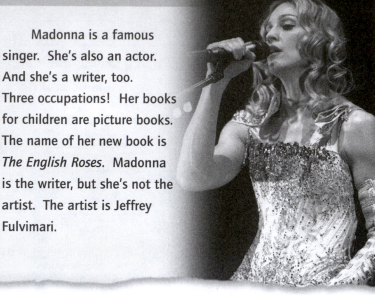

Madonna is a famous singer. She's also an actor. And she's a writer, too. Three occupations! Her books for children are picture books. The name of her new book is *The English Roses*. Madonna is the writer, but she's not the artist. The artist is Jeffrey Fulvimari.

Now answer the questions. Check ✔ the boxes.

1. What are Madonna's occupations?

☐ artist ☐ photographer ☐ teacher

☐ actor ☐ singer ☐ writer

2. What is Jeffrey Fulvimari's occupation?

☐ photographer ☐ teacher ☐ artist

9 ▷ **Circle the occupation that is not spelled correctly.**

1. engineer	lawyer	arkitect	athlete
2. shef	banker	teacher	singer
3. scientist	fotografer	musician	manager
4. writer	nurse	actor	flite attendant

Now write the words correctly.

5. _____

6. _____

7. _____

8. _____

LESSON 3

10 Rewrite the sentences. Use capital letters to begin the proper nouns.

1. john landry is a chef in paris.

   _____.

2. isabel hunter is from canada. She's an architect.

   _____.

3. alex quinn is a pilot. He's in tokyo today.

   _____.

11 Read the occupations in the box. Count the syllables. Write each occupation in the correct place on the chart.

| athlete | chef | ~~engineer~~ | lawyer | manager | musician |
| nurse | photographer | scientist | singer | writer | |

1 syllable	2 syllables	3 syllables	4 syllables
		engineer	

12 Choose the correct response. Circle the letter.

1. How are you?

   a. I'm Samantha.   **b.** Great.   **c.** Take care.

2. What do you do?

   a. I'm a manager.   **b.** Fine, thanks.   **c.** I'm Jim.

3. Are you Lucy?

   a. Yes, she is.   **b.** Nice to meet you, Lucy.   **c.** No, I'm not.

4. How do you spell that?

   a. Right over there.   **b.** D-E-N-Z-E-L.   **c.** I'm a writer. And you?

A RIDDLE FOR YOU!

Ms. Adams, Ms. Banks, Ms. Clark, and Ms. Dare have four different occupations—
engineer, **architect**, **doctor**, and **lawyer** (but NOT in that order).

Read the statements.

Ms. Adams and Ms. Clark are not doctors.
Ms. Banks and Ms. Clark are not lawyers.
Ms. Clark and Ms. Dare are not architects.
Ms. Adams is not a lawyer.

Now write an occupation for each person.

Ms. Adams: _____

Ms. Banks: _____

Ms. Clark: _____

Ms. Dare: _____

SOURCE: Adapted from www.norfolkacademy.org.

2 **WORD FIND. Look across (→) and down (↓). Circle the eight occupations.
Then write the occupations on the lines.**

_____

_____

_____

_____

_____

_____

_____

_____

N	E	I	M	E	P	A	E	N	N	B	K	R	P	P	E
M	O	E	T	E	O	A	M	E	S	U	I	H	A	T	L
A	E	L	P	O	L	L	H	N	C	N	N	N	T	R	Y
N	T	L	E	S	A	A	S	A	I	H	H	R	R	L	I
A	O	A	H	T	E	T	T	R	E	T	E	T	E	N	C
G	K	W	E	N	P	H	E	S	N	A	H	N	E	S	A
E	N	Y	P	C	R	L	A	M	T	R	E	N	S	R	E
R	T	E	A	E	A	E	I	N	I	N	N	E	R	N	U
K	A	R	A	S	H	T	A	A	S	E	R	E	R	A	T
O	N	T	N	Y	T	E	I	U	T	E	H	G	R	N	M
E	U	P	H	O	T	O	G	R	A	P	H	E	R	H	E
R	R	N	A	S	M	B	E	N	G	I	N	E	E	R	B
N	S	E	N	R	A	E	E	E	E	R	A	E	R	E	L
A	E	O	K	P	E	G	N	E	R	A	N	U	U	H	E
O	T	T	B	A	N	K	E	R	T	L	E	G	C	T	E
N	N	K	R	N	N	E	R	N	R	T	B	I	G	E	T

SOURCE: Created with www.spellbuilder.com.

UNIT 2

Relationships

LESSON 1

1 Look at the pictures. Write possessive adjectives.

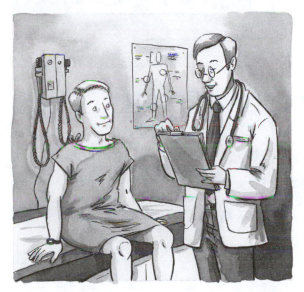

1. _His_ doctor is Dr. Brown.

2. _____ teacher is Ms. Jalbert.

3. _____ boss is Mr. Lin.

4. _____ neighbors are Mr. and Mrs. Rivers.

2 Look at the pictures. Complete the sentences about relationships.
Use possessive nouns.

Eric

1. They are _Eric's classmates_____.

Lucy

2. She is _____.

Jack

3. They are _____.

Edwin

4. He is _____.

3 Match the description and the relationship. Write the letter on the line.

1. ____ Caleb and Isabel are managers. Their company
   is Infotech. Their boss is Mr. Jackson.

2. ____ You're a student. Joan is a student, too.
   Ms. Lewis is your teacher and Joan's teacher, too.

3. ____ Jessica and I are classmates. She's my neighbor, too.

a. You're classmates.

b. They're colleagues.

c. We're friends.

4 Complete the sentences.

1. Sally is _____ classmate.
   <u>I / my</u>

2. We're _____ students.
   <u>Mr. Haber's / Mr. Haber</u>

3. Who is _____ teacher?
   <u>you / your</u>

4. Ms. Miller and Mr. Sullivan are _____ colleagues.
   <u>our / we</u>

5. Are _____ neighbors?
   <u>they / their</u>

6. Dr. Franklin isn't _____ doctor.
   <u>Bill / Bill's</u>

5 Look at Joe's list and Amy's list for their party.

JOE'S LIST
Kristin – friend
Jeff – friend
Robert and Julie – friends
Mark – classmate
Gary and Ann – neighbors

Amy's list
Samantha — colleague
Peter — colleague
Katherine — boss
Gary and Ann — neighbors
Robert and Julie — friends

Now write sentences about the people. Use possessive adjectives.

1. Peter: *Peter is her colleague*   .

2. Mark: _____.

3. Gary and Ann: _____.

4. Katherine: _____.

5. Kristin: _____.

6 YOUR RELATIONSHIPS. **Complete the chart with names.**

Classmates or Colleagues	Neighbors	Friends

7 **Choose a friend and a classmate from Exercise 6. Introduce them. Complete the conversation.**

1. You: _____, this is _____.
   _____'s my classmate.

2. Your friend: Hi, _____.

3. Your classmate: Hi, _____. Nice to meet you.
   Your friend: Nice to meet you, too.
   Your classmate: What do you do?

4. Your friend: I'm _____. And you?

5. Your classmate: I'm _____.

LESSON 2

8 ▸ **Fill out the forms for the people.**

1. Your teacher

☐ Mr.
☐ Mrs. _____ _____
☐ Miss _____*first name*_____ _____*last name*_____
☐ Ms.

2. A classmate

☐ Mr.
☐ Mrs. _____ _____
☐ Miss _____*first name*_____ _____*last name*_____
☐ Ms.

3. A neighbor

☐ Mr.
☐ Mrs. _____ _____
☐ Miss _____*first name*_____ _____*last name*_____
☐ Ms.

4. A friend

☐ Mr.
☐ Mrs. _____ _____
☐ Miss _____*first name*_____ _____*last name*_____
☐ Ms.

9 ▸ **Choose one person from Exercise 8. Complete the conversation between the person and a clerk.**

1. **Clerk:** What's your last name, please?

   _____: _____.

2. **Clerk:** And your first name?

   _____: _____.

3. **Clerk:** How do you spell that?

   _____: _____.

4. **Clerk:** Thank you, _____.

   _____: _____.

LESSON 3

10 ▸ **Complete the address book with information for three friends.**

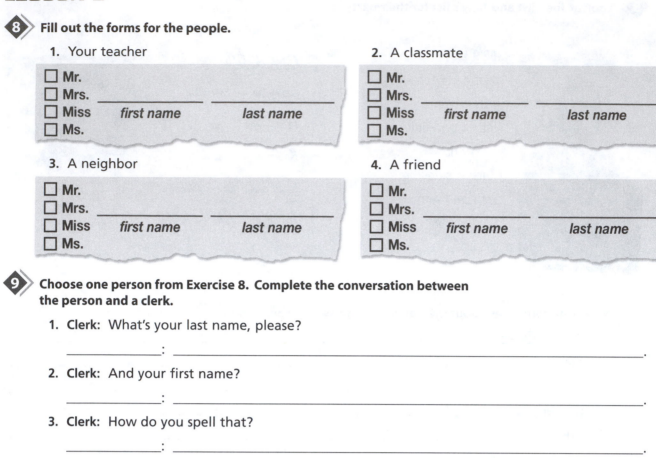

1	2	3
Last name First name	Last name First name	Last name First name
Address	Address	Address
Phone number	Phone number	Phone number
Cell-phone number	Cell-phone number	Cell-phone number
E-mail address	E-mail address	E-mail address

11 ▸ **Write the answers in words.**

1. eleven + six = _____
2. nineteen − twelve = _____
3. three × five = _____
4. twenty ÷ two = _____

12 ▸ **Look at the business cards. Read the responses. Then write questions with**
What's. Use possessive nouns or possessive adjectives.

Jeff Silver
Manager

EDI International

215 East 11th Street
New York, NY 10003
TEL (212) 555–0769
FAX (212) 555–0770
jeff.silver@edi.com

Kate Harrison

Architect
Foster & Wright
77 York St.
Sydney NSW 2000
(61–2) 9262–1036
kharrison@fosterwright.com

Michael Brent

Engineer

28 Manor Street

London E17

0208 755 8050

1. **A:** *What's Ms. Harrison's first name* ? **B:** Kate.
2. **A:** *What's her address* ? **B:** 77 York St.
3. **A:** _____ ? **B:** jeff.silver@edi.com.
4. **A:** _____ ? **B:** Manager.
5. **A:** _____ ? **B:** 0208 755 8050.
6. **A:** _____ ? **B:** 28 Manor Street.

13 ▸ **WHAT ABOUT YOU? Answer the questions.**

1. What's your first name? _____.
2. What's your last name? _____.
3. What's your occupation? _____.
4. What's your address? _____.
5. What's your phone number? _____.
6. Cell phone? Check ✔ yes or no. Yes ☐ No ☐
   What's your cell-phone number? _____.
7. E-mail? Check ✔ yes or no. Yes ☐ No ☐
   What's your e-mail address? _____.

JUST FOR **FUN**

1 ▷ TAKE A GUESS! **Write the next number in words.**

1. three, six, nine, twelve, fifteen, _____

2. one, two, four, eight, _____

3. twenty, one, nineteen, two, eighteen, three, _____

Source: From www.riddlenut.com.

2 ▷ **Complete the puzzle.**

Across

4. We are _____. Our addresses are 15 and 17 Pine Street.

5. The Musee du Louvre's _____ is 99 Rue de Rivoli, Paris.

9. I.M. Pei's occupation

10. Her name is Linda Reid. Reid is her _____ name.

Down

1. Mr. Bryant is Andy's teacher. Andy is _____ student.

2. Their address is 11 Palm Street, and their _____ is (661) 555–4485.

3. Isabel Allende's title

6. Allison's _____ address is allie@mail.net.

7. Flight attendants and pilots are _____.

8. A=one, B=two, C=three, . . . N=_____

Source: Created with Discovery's Puzzlemaker.

Guess: 1. eighteen; 2. sixteen; 3. seventeen

UNIT 3

Directions and Transportation

LESSON 1

 Write the names of places in your community.

1. a restaurant: _____

2. a bank: _____

3. a bookstore: _____

4. a convenience store: _____

5. a travel agency: _____

6. a pharmacy: _____

 Read the directions. Label the places on the map.

- The post office is across the street.

- The bookstore is around the corner.

- The bank is next to the bookstore.

- The newsstand is down the street on the left.

- The travel agency is down the street on the right.

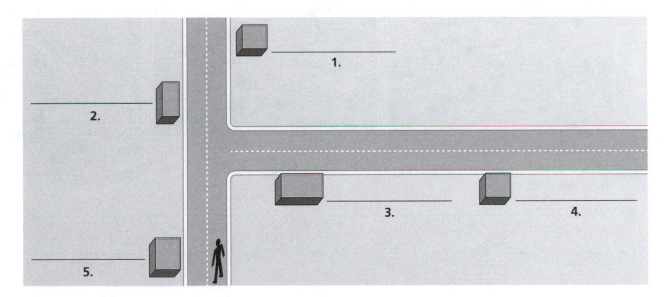

3 ▷ **Read the answers. Then complete the questions with <u>Where's</u> or <u>What's</u>.**

1. A: _____ the address?   B: 214 New Street.

2. A: _____ the bookstore?   B: It's down the street on the left.

3. A: _____ the pharmacy?   B: It's across the street.

4. A: _____ Lisa's occupation?   B: She's a lawyer.

5. A: _____ his e-mail address?   B: Rob123@mail.net.

6. A: _____ your friend's restaurant?   B: It's around the corner.

4 ▷ **WHAT ABOUT YOU? Answer the questions.**

1. What's your address? _____.

2. Is there a newsstand near your home? _____.

3. Is there a convenience store near your home? _____.

4. Is there a bank near your home? _____.

5. Is there a post office near your home? _____.

5 ▷ **Describe the location of one place near <u>your</u> home.**

Example: *The convenience store is around the corner* _____.

_____.

LESSON 2

6 ▷ **HOW DO I GET TO . . . ? Write directions from <u>your</u> home to one place in <u>your</u> community.**

Start: _____
                                   (your address)

_____.

_____.

_____.

_____.

_____.

End: _____
                          (a place in your community)

Look at the map. Then follow the directions.

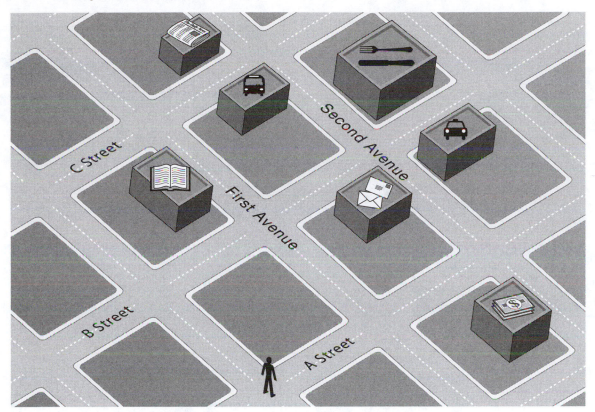

1. Go two blocks and turn left.

   Go to the corner of B Street and Second Avenue.

   Turn right at the corner.

   It's on the left.

   Where are you? _____.

2. Go to the corner of A Street and First Avenue.

   Turn left.

   Go two blocks and turn right.

   Go straight.

   It's on the right.

   Where are you? _____.

LESSON 3

 Match the occupations and the places.

1. ____ an athlete   a. an airport

2. ____ a clerk   b. a restaurant

3. ____ a chef   c. a bank

4. ____ a banker   d. a convenience store

5. ____ a pilot   e. a stadium

9 **Look at the pictures. What is the place? Write a sentence.**

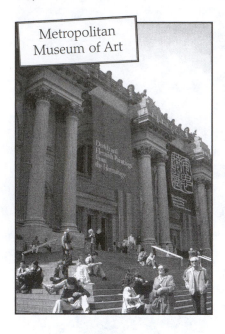

Metropolitan Museum of Art

Central Park

Grand Central Terminal

1. _It's a museum_ .   2. _____ .   3. _____ .

John F. Kennedy International Airport

Tavern on the Green

4. _____ .   5. _____ .

Yankee Stadium

6. _____ .

10 Choose a city. Write the names of places in the city.

What city is it? _____

1. a train station: _____

2. an airport: _____

3. a stadium: _____

4. a park: _____

5. a museum: _____

6. a restaurant: _____

11 WHAT ABOUT YOU? Answer the questions.

1. What's your favorite museum? _____

2. What's your favorite park? _____

3. What's your favorite mall? _____

4. What's your favorite stadium? _____

5. What's your favorite restaurant? _____

6. What's your favorite pharmacy? _____

12 Give advice to visitors in your community. Choose a place. Suggest a means of transportation. Use an affirmative imperative and a negative imperative.

1. "How do I get to the _____?"   YOU _____.
   (airport or train station or bus station)   _____.

2. "How do I get to the _____?"   YOU _____.
   (mall or stadium or park)   _____.

3. "How do I get to the _____?"   YOU _____.
   (museum or travel agency or bookstore)   _____.

4. "How do I get to the _____?"   YOU _____.
   (pharmacy or taxi stand or post office)   _____.

1 A RIDDLE FOR YOU! **Read the clues. Then write the places on the lines.**

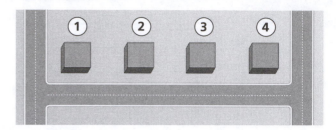

- The travel agency is not on the corner.
- The bank is not next to the travel agency.
- The post office is next to the bank.
- The pharmacy is not on the left corner.

1. _____

2. _____

3. _____

4. _____

2 WORD FIND. **Look across (→) and down (↓). Circle the fifteen places. Then write the places on the lines.**

_____

_____

_____

_____

_____

_____

_____

_____

_____

_____

_____

_____

_____

_____

_____

P	R	R	T	I	T	N	M	E	C	F	F	K	P	I	A
B	A	N	K	I	B	U	S	S	T	A	T	I	O	N	U
O	R	T	R	A	V	E	L	A	G	E	N	C	Y	T	O
N	E	P	O	S	T	O	F	F	I	C	E	S	M	T	O
A	S	N	E	W	S	T	A	N	D	P	T	S	R	F
E	T	T	I	T	E	F	N	I	B	M	H	A	O	A	Y
K	A	A	A	M	A	L	L	L	O	E	A	D	S	I	F
A	U	X	A	M	S	M	M	T	O	E	R	I	A	N	A
A	R	I	N	K	T	U	N	R	K	P	M	U	I	S	A
T	A	S	O	O	T	S	N	B	S	A	A	M	R	T	N
G	N	T	S	B	U	E	B	E	T	R	C	B	P	A	P
I	T	A	O	S	O	U	A	S	O	K	Y	G	O	T	Y
A	T	N	M	T	A	M	R	A	R	M	T	E	R	I	R
A	M	D	T	U	A	A	E	T	E	E	A	N	T	O	O
M	S	A	T	N	I	H	H	O	O	M	Y	H	T	N	N
S	U	O	E	A	R	A	A	A	N	T	T	S	O	T	I

SOURCE: Created with www.spellbuilder.com.

People

1 THE BRITISH ROYAL FAMILY. **Write the family member's relationship to Queen Elizabeth on the line.**

Queen Elizabeth ——————— Prince Philip
1. *her husband*

Prince Charles

Princess Anne

Prince Andrew

Prince Edward

2. _____

3. _____

Prince William

Prince Harry

Peter Phillips

Zara Phillips

Princess Beatrice

Princess Eugenie

Lady Louise Windsor

4. _____

5. _____

2 **Look at Queen Elizabeth's family again. Complete the sentences.**

1. Prince Harry is Prince William's _____.

2. Princess Anne is Zara Phillips's _____.

3. Queen Elizabeth and Prince Philip are Prince Charles's _____.

4. Prince Philip is Prince Harry's _____.

5. Queen Elizabeth is Prince Philip's _____.

6. Prince William and Prince Harry are Prince Charles's _____.

7. Prince Andrew is Princess Eugenie's _____.

8. Queen Elizabeth is Peter Phillips's _____.

9. Princess Eugenie is Princess Beatrice's _____.

10. William, Harry, Peter, Zara, Beatrice, Eugenie, and Louise are Queen Elizabeth's _____.

3 **Complete the conversation. Write <u>What</u>, <u>Where</u>, or <u>Who</u>.**

1. **Andrew:** _____'s that?

 Hannah: That's my brother.

2. **Andrew:** _____'s your brother's first name?

 Hannah: Paul.

3. **Andrew:** _____'s your sister?

 Hannah: She's right there, on the left.

4. **Andrew:** _____'s that?

 Hannah: My grandmother.

5. **Andrew:** _____'s her last name?

 Hannah: Connor.

6. **Andrew:** _____ are your parents?

 Hannah: They're here, next to my grandmother.

4 **Read the answers. Then write questions with <u>Who</u>.**

1. **A:** _____?

 B: They're my brothers.

2. **A:** _____?

 B: That's my husband.

3. **A:** _____?

 B: He's my father.

4. **A:** _____?

 B: They're my grandparents.

5. **A:** _____?

 B: She's my sister.

5 **WHAT ABOUT YOU?** **Answer the questions.**

1. Who are you? _____.

2. Who's your teacher? _____.

3. Who are your classmates? (Name three.) _____

 _____.

LESSON 2

 6 **Look at the photos and read.**

> Hi, I'm Kate. There are five people in my family. I have two sisters. Their names are Megan and Jane. Jane and I are students. Megan is a doctor.

> Hello. My name is Edgar. My wife's name is Anna. I'm an engineer, and she's an architect. We have two children. Riley is our son, and Reese is our daughter.

> Hello. I'm George. My wife Carol and I are grandparents. We have three children and two grandchildren. Our granddaughter is Sophia. Our grandson is Jake.

Now answer the questions.

1. Who's Jake? _He's George's grandson_____.

2. Who's Anna? _____.

3. Who's Jane? _____.

4. Who are Riley and Reese? _____.

5. Who are George and Carol? _____.

6. Who's a doctor? _____.

 7 **Look at the picture. Write sentences with <u>have</u> or <u>has</u>.**

1. Julia: _She has two brothers_____.

2. Rose: _____.

3. Barbara and Martin: _____.

4. Dan and Michael: _____.

5. Louis: _____.

8 **Write the numbers in words.**

1. twenty-one, twenty-eight, thirty-five, forty-two, _____

2. four, eight, sixteen, _____, sixty-four

3. ninety-nine, _____, seventy-five, sixty-three, fifty-one

4. ten, eleven, twenty-one, thirty-two, fifty-three, _____

9 **Complete each sentence with <u>have</u> or <u>has</u>. Then choose the correct response. Circle the letter.**

1. Matthew _____ two sisters.

   a. How old is she?   **b.** How old are they?

2. Mark and Jamie _____ a daughter.

   a. How old is he?   **b.** How old is she?

3. I _____ a brother and a sister.

   a. How old is your brother?   **b.** How old is my sister?

4. We _____ a son.

   a. What's your name?   **b.** What's his name?

10 **Choose four people from the box.**

mother	father	sister	daughter	husband
brother	grandmother	grandfather	wife	son

Now answer questions about <u>your</u> family.

1. How old is your _____? _____.

2. How old is your _____? _____.

3. How old is your _____? _____.

4. How old is your _____? _____.

5. How old are you? _____.

LESSON 3

11 **Write the names of three family members, friends, neighbors, or classmates. Then complete the chart.**

Name	Relationship	Age	Occupation	pretty	handsome	cute	short	tall	old	young
Michelle	sister	26	manager	✔				✔		✔

12 Unscramble the words. Write sentences.

1. brother / tall / is / My / very <u>My brother is very tall</u>   .

2. handsome, / He / too / very / is _____.

3. your / Are / pretty / sisters _____?

4. is / daughter / young / Her _____.

5. cute / so / is / She _____!

13 Answer the questions. Use famous people.

1. Who's tall? <u>Shaquille O'Neal is tall</u>   .

2. Who's old? _____.

3. Who's good-looking? _____.

4. Who's young? _____.

5. Who's short? _____.

6. Who's cute? _____.

14 Write sentences about <u>your</u> family.

JUST FOR FUN

1 **A RIDDLE FOR YOU!** **Read the sentence. Then answer the question.**

Brothers and sisters have I none, but that man's father is my father's son.

Who is "that man"? _____

SOURCE: From thinks.com.

2 **Complete the puzzle.**

Across

3. Not tall

5. His daughter's son is his _____.

7. Her grandchildren are very ____.
   They're one and three years old.

9. Alejandro Fernandez's father

10. The English alphabet has _____ letters.

11. Venus and Serena Williams are _____.

Down

1. Michelle has two daughters and a son.
   She has three _____.

2. Julie's grandmother is ninety-two.
   She's _____.

4. A good-looking man is _____.

6. My father's mother is my _____.

8. A good-looking woman is _____.

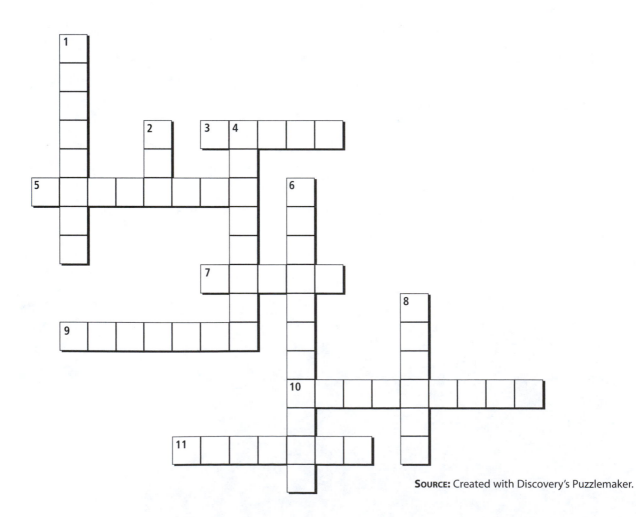

SOURCE: Created with Discovery's Puzzlemaker.

Riddle: My son

Events and Times

LESSON 1

 Match the times.

1. __c__ It's half past ten.
2. ____ It's four o'clock.
3. ____ It's noon.
4. ____ It's a quarter after two.
5. ____ It's five to nine.
6. ____ It's six ten.
7. ____ It's a quarter to seven.
8. ____ It's midnight.

a. 6:45
b. 8:55
c. 10:30
d. 12:00 P.M.
e. 4:00
f. 6:10
g. 12:00 A.M.
h. 2:15

 Look at the pictures. Are the people <u>early</u>, <u>late</u>, or <u>on time</u>?

DATE:
AUGUST 4
FROM:
NEW YORK
TO:
WASHINGTON
TIME:
9:17 P.M.

DATE:
AUGUST 4
FROM:
NEW YORK
TO:
BOSTON
TIME:
8:30 P.M.

DATE:
AUGUST 4
FROM:
NEW YORK
TO:
PHILADELPHIA
TIME:
8:15 P.M.

1. _____

2. _____

3. _____

Look at the pictures. Then complete the conversation.

LESSON 2

4 **Write an occupation for each event.**

1. a speech: *a writer*
2. a movie: _____
3. a game: _____
4. a concert: _____
5. a play: _____

5 **When is your English class? Circle the day or days. Write the times.**

Monday	Tuesday	Wednesday	Thursday	Friday	Saturday	Sunday

6 **What events are in your city or town this week? Complete the chart.**

Name	Event	Day	Time	Place
Yo-Yo Ma	Concert	Saturday	7:00 P.M.	Music Center

7 Look at the posters.

Now check ✔ <u>true</u> or <u>false</u>.

	true	false
1. The game is on Sunday.	☐	☐
2. The movie is at 7:10 on Wednesday.	☐	☐
3. The play is at half past seven.	☐	☐
4. The concert is at three o'clock.	☐	☐
5. The movie is at 3:40 on Saturday.	☐	☐

8 Look at the posters in Exercise 7 again. Read the answers. Then write the questions.

1. **A:** _____? **B:** One o'clock.

2. **A:** _____? **B:** Tuesday at a quarter to eight.

3. **A:** _____? **B:** Thursday.

4. **A:** _____? **B:** City Park.

9 Invite a friend to one of the events. Look at the times and days on the posters in Exercise 7.

1. **You:** Hi, _____. How are you?

   Your friend: Fine, thanks. And you?

2. **You:** _____.

   There's a _____ on _____ — _____.

   Would you like to go?

   Your friend: Sounds great. What time?

3. **You:** _____.

   Your friend: OK. Let's meet at _____.

LESSON 3

 Complete the sentences. Write a family member or a relationship and then a month.

1. My _mother's_ birthday is in _January_ .
2. My _____ birthday is in _____ .
3. My _____ birthday is in _____ .
4. My _____ birthday is in _____ .
5. My _____ birthday is in _____ .

11 **Look at the pictures. Write the months for each type of weather where you live.**

1. _____
2. _____
3. _____

12 **Complete the conversations. Use the prepositions <u>in</u>, <u>on</u>, and <u>at</u>.**

1. **A:** When's your birthday?   **B:** ____ May. It's ____ May 11th.

2. **A:** How do I get to the bus station?   **B:** Turn left ____ the corner.

3. **A:** Am I late?   **B:** No, you're ____ time.

4. **A:** What time is the speech?   **B:** It's ____ 1:30.

5. **A:** Is the class at 9:15 A.M.?   **B:** No, it's ____ the afternoon, ____ 3:45.

6. **A:** Where's the convenience store?   **B:** Down the street, ____ the right.

7. **A:** Is the restaurant near here?   **B:** Yes, it's ____ Grove Street.

8. **A:** When is the party?   **B:** ____ Friday, ____ noon, ____ Mike's house.

13 ▸ **Look at the invitation.**

Now answer the questions. Write complete sentences.

1. What month is the party? _It's in March_ .
2. What date is the party? _____ .
3. What day is the party? _____ .
4. What time is the party? _____ .
5. Where's the party? _____ .
6. Where's the restaurant? _____ .

1 Fill in the answers. Then look at the numbers under the lines. Write the letters in the puzzle.

1. A play, concert, or speech.

$\underline{\quad}\ \underline{\quad}_{12}\ \underline{\quad}_{3}\ \underline{\quad}_{10}\ \underline{\quad}\ \underline{\quad}\ \underline{\quad}\ \underline{\quad}_{1}$

2. The class is on weekdays—Mondays, Wednesdays, and _____.

$\underline{\quad}_{8}\ \underline{\quad}_{4}\ \underline{\quad}_{5}\ \underline{\quad}\ \underline{\quad}\ \underline{\quad}_{11}\ \underline{\quad}_{6}$

3. An event with athletes.

$\underline{\quad}\ \underline{\quad}_{13}\ \underline{\quad}\ \underline{\quad}_{7}\ \underline{\quad}$

4. April is the _____ month of the year.

$\underline{\quad}_{9}\ \underline{\quad}\ \underline{\quad}\ \underline{\quad}\ \underline{\quad}_{2}$

Puzzle

" $\underline{\quad}_{1}\ \underline{\quad}_{2}\ \underline{\quad}_{3}\ \underline{\quad}_{4}\ \underline{\quad}_{3}\quad \underline{\quad}_{5}\ \underline{\quad}_{6}\quad \underline{\quad}_{1}\ \underline{\quad}_{5}\ \underline{\quad}_{7}\ \underline{\quad}_{3}\quad \underline{\quad}_{8}\ \underline{\quad}_{9}\ \underline{\quad}_{4}\quad \underline{\quad}_{3}\ \underline{\quad}_{10}\ \underline{\quad}_{3}\ \underline{\quad}_{4}\ \underline{\quad}_{11}\ \underline{\quad}_{1}\ \underline{\quad}_{2}\ \underline{\quad}_{5}\ \underline{\quad}_{12}\ \underline{\quad}_{13}$. "

—Thomas Edison, inventor (U.S.)

2 Complete the puzzle.

Across

5. This month has twenty-eight days.

7. Jana's birthday is March 12th. What's her sign?

9. The movie's at 10:15. It's a quarter to ten now. You're _____.

10. Good _____! (at 7:00 P.M.)

13. Good _____! (at 7:00 A.M.)

Down

1. The ninth month of the year

2. The fourth weekday

3. The first day of the weekend

4. The time in London when it's 4:30 P.M. in Mexico City

6. Q is the _____ letter in the alphabet.

8. The _____ is at the stadium.

11. 12:00 A.M.

12. 12:00 P.M.

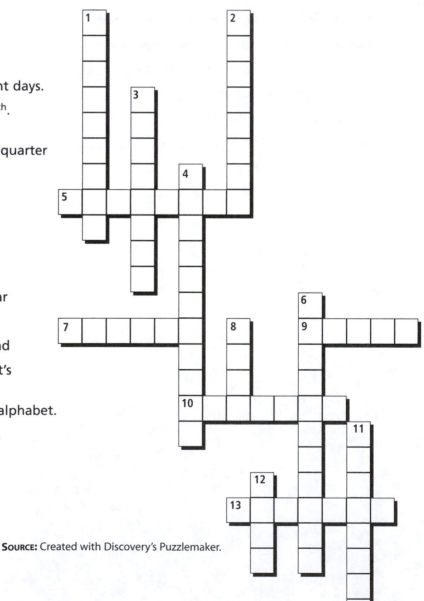

SOURCE: Created with Discovery's Puzzlemaker.

Clothes

LESSON 1

1 Write the name of the clothes.

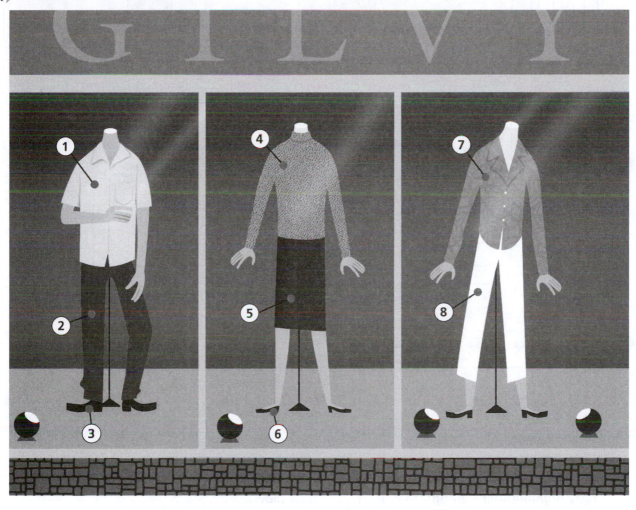

1. _____
2. _____
3. _____
4. _____
5. _____
6. _____
7. _____
8. _____

2 **Circle one of the clothing items in each picture. Write a sentence with I like and this, that, these, or those.**

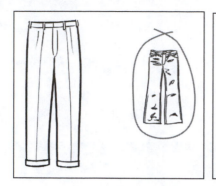  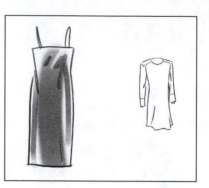

Example: _I like those pants_ . **1.** _____ **2.** _____

_____ . _____ .

3. _____ **4.** _____

_____ . _____ .

3 **Write sentences. Use words from each box.**

| I
My sister / brother
My friend and I
My classmate
My neighbors
My friends
My grandmother / grandfather
My teacher | + | like
likes | + | restaurants
bookstores
malls
parks
museums
movies
plays
parties |

1. _My friends like parties_ _____ .

2. _____ .

3. _____ .

4. _____ .

5. _____ .

4 ▸ **Look at the pictures. Compliment each person on his or her clothes.**

1. _____

_____

_____

2. _____

_____

_____

LESSON 2

5 ▸ **Complete the sentences. Write the simple present tense of the verb.**

1. My daughters _____ those dresses.
   want

2. Susan's friend _____ her skirt.
   not like

3. Michael and Steven _____ suits.
   not have

4. _____ you _____ a jacket?
   have

5. We _____ shoes for the party.
   need

6. _____ Anthony _____ this tie?
   want

6 ▸ **Look at the clothes. Complete the questions. Then answer the questions for yourself.**

1. Do you like _*these shoes*_____? _____.
2. Do you like _____? _____.
3. Do you like _____? _____.
4. Do you like _____? _____.

LESSON 3

 7 **Plan your clothes for next week. Write on the calendar.**

Monday	Tuesday	Wednesday	Thursday	Friday	Saturday	Sunday
gray pants						
black sweater						
new black shoes						

8 **Write sentences about yourself. Use <u>have</u> / <u>don't have</u>, <u>want</u> / <u>don't want</u>, or <u>need</u> / <u>don't need</u>.**

Example: brown shoes: *I want new brown shoes* _____ .

1. a blue suit: _____ .

2. a red sweater: _____ .

3. a white shirt / blouse: _____ .

4. a black jacket: _____ .

5. gray pants: _____ .

9 **Read about Elena and Marina's shopping trip.**

   Elena and Marina are sisters. They're at the mall on Market Street. They need clothes for work. Elena is a manager, and Marina is a musician. Elena's suit is old, and she needs a new one. She wants new shoes, too. Marina needs a black dress for a concert on Saturday.

   At their favorite store, Lily's Clothes, there are a black suit, a gray suit, a brown suit, and a red suit. Elena likes the gray suit. But the store doesn't have shoes. Marina likes a purple dress, but she doesn't need a purple dress.

Now read the answers. Then write questions.

1. **A:** _____ ? **B:** New shoes.

2. **A:** _____ ? **B:** Marina does.

3. **A:** _____ ? **B:** On Saturday.

4. **A:** _____ ? **B:** The gray suit.

10 Choose the words to complete the conversation. Write the letter on the line.

1. **A:** Let's go shopping for Cecilia's birthday.

   B: _____

2. **A:** A new sweater.

   B: _____

3. **A:** No, she doesn't.

   B: _____

4. **A:** She already has a red sweater.

   B: _____

   A: It's beautiful! And she doesn't have a blue sweater.

a. How about red?

b. Does she like orange?

c. I think this blue sweater is very nice.

d. OK. What does she want?

11 Complete the conversation. Use your <u>own</u> words.

1. "I like this suit. Do you?"

   YOU _____.

2. "And which tie do you like?"

   YOU _____.

3. "I like it, too. Do you like these shoes?"

   YOU _____.

4. "I really like shopping!"

   YOU _____.

TAKE A GUESS! **Match the numbers with the letters to make these colors.**

1. ___ green   **a.** red and green
2. ___ orange   **b.** yellow and blue
3. ___ purple   **c.** yellow and red
4. ___ brown   **d.** black and white
5. ___ gray   **e.** blue and red

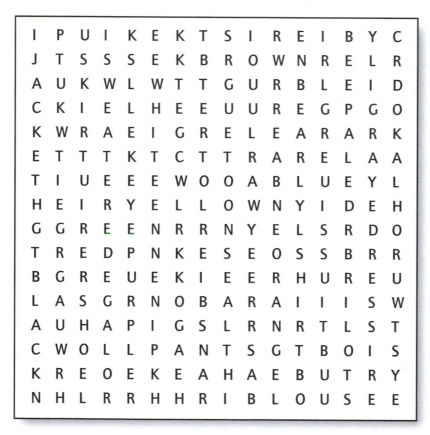 **WORD FIND.** **Look across (→) and down (↓). Circle the ten clothes and the ten colors. Then write the clothes and colors on the lines.**

```
I P U I K E K T S I R E I B Y C
J T S S E K B R O W N R E L R
A U K W L W T T G U R B L E I D
C K I E L H E E U U R E G P G O
K W R A E I G R E L E A R A R K
E T T T K T C T T R A R E L A A
T I U E E W O O A B L U E Y L
H E I R Y E L L O W N Y I D E H
G G R E E N R R N Y E L S R D O
T R E D P N K E S E O S S B R R
B G R E U E K I E E R H U R E U
L A S G R N O B A R A I I S W
A U H A P I G S L R N R T L S T
C W O L L P A N T S G T B O I S
K R E O E K E A H A E B U T R Y
N H L R R H H R I B L O U S E E
```

Source: Created with www.spellbuilder.com.

Clothes		Colors	
_____	_____	_____	_____
_____	_____	_____	_____
_____	_____	_____	_____
_____	_____	_____	_____
_____	_____	_____	_____

Home and Work

LESSON 1

  Match the occupations and the workplaces.

1. _____ a teacher   **a.** a hospital

2. _____ a nurse   **b.** an office

3. _____ a chef   **c.** a school

4. _____ a manager   **d.** an airport

5. _____ a flight attendant **e.** a restaurant

② Read about the friends and neighbors. Then write their names on the lines.

- Dr. Pierce lives in a house on New Street. It's between Orange Avenue and Green Avenue.

- Mr. and Mrs. Hunter live at 21 Green Avenue. Their house is across from the school.

- Diana's apartment is at the corner of New Street and Orange Avenue, near the convenience store. She lives on the first floor.

- Carla lives on Orange Avenue, around the corner from Dr. Pierce.

- Charles lives across from Dr. Pierce and around the corner from Mr. and Mrs. Hunter. His house has a nice garden.

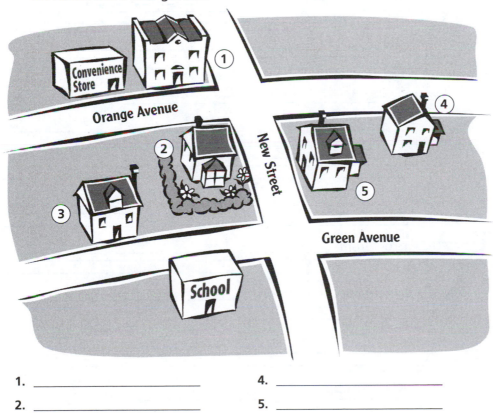

1. _____   4. _____

2. _____   5. _____

3. _____

3 Complete the conversations. Use the prepositions <u>in</u>, <u>on</u>, and <u>at</u>.

1. **A:** Where do you live?   **B:** _____ an apartment.

2. **A:** Is there an elevator?   **B:** No, but it's OK. I live _____ the first floor.

3. **A:** Are you a student?   **B:** Yes, I study _____ the English School.

4. **A:** Do you live near the school?   **B:** Yes, _____ Third Avenue.

5. **A:** Where do you work?   **B:** _____ an office. I'm a manager.

6. **A:** Where does your wife work?   **B:** She works _____ home. She's a writer.

7. **A:** What about your son?   **B:** He works _____ Center Restaurant. He's a chef.

8. **A:** Does he live near the restaurant? **B:** No, he lives _____ Bank Street.

4 Complete the charts with all the places that apply to you.

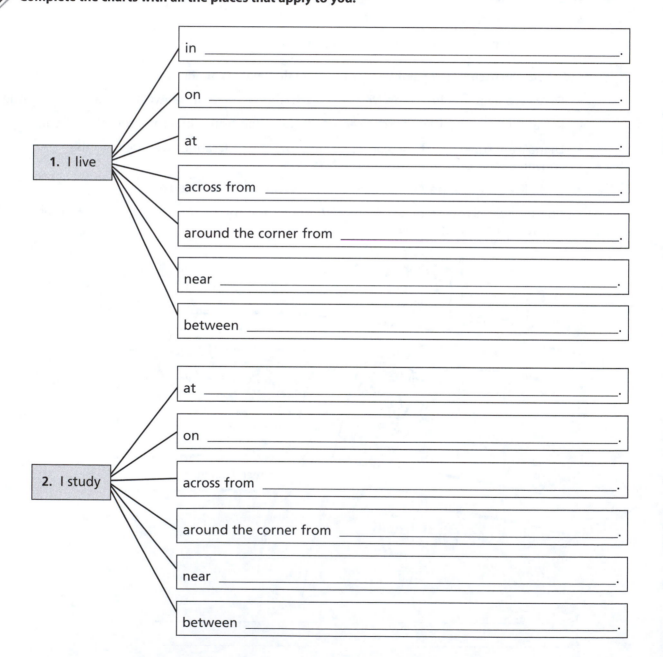

1. I live

in _____ .

on _____ .

at _____ .

across from _____ .

around the corner from _____ .

near _____ .

between _____ .

2. I study

at _____ .

on _____ .

across from _____ .

around the corner from _____ .

near _____ .

between _____ .

5 Complete the information about your home.

1 Circle one:

house

apartment

3 How many do you have in your home?

bathroom(s) _____ bedroom(s) _____ closet(s) _____

2 Check ✔ the rooms in your home.

☐ kitchen
☐ living room
☐ dining room
☐ bedroom(s)

4 Check ✔ yes or no. Does your home have . . .

	yes	no
a garden?	☐	☐
a garage?	☐	☐
a balcony?	☐	☐
a large kitchen?	☐	☐
a second floor?	☐	☐

6 Write an ad for your home.

WORLD SEARCH

Live in a house or apartment overseas for 1-6 months!   Telephone: 1-800-555-9038 E-mail: worldsearch@pcb.com

1. Available in Paris (France)

Two-bedroom house with large kitchen   Two-bedroom apartment with small kitchen

2. Available in Buenos Aires (Argentina)

Two-bedroom house with two bathrooms   Three-bedroom house with three bathrooms

3. Available in Tokyo (Japan)

One-bedroom apartment with large closets   One-bedroom apartment with large kitchen

4. Available in Montreal (Canada)

Two-bedroom house with large garden   Two-bedroom apartment with balcony

5.

7 Look at Exercise 6 again. Circle the ad for a house or an apartment you like. Describe the home to a friend. Write complete sentences.

Example: _It's a house. It's in Paris. There are two bedrooms._ _____

_____

_____

Now write two questions to ask about the house or apartment. Use Is there, Are there, or How many.

1. _____?

2. _____?

LESSON 3

 8 Look at the floor plans for two apartments. What are they like? Write four sentences with __There is__ and four sentences with __There are__.

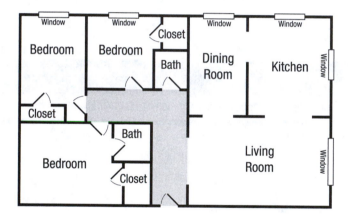

1. _There is one bedroom_____.

2. _____.

3. _____.

4. _____.

5. _____.

6. _There are three bedrooms_____.

7. _____.

8. _____.

9. _____.

10. _____.

9 What new furniture or appliances do you want for your home? Make a list of four items you want.

Example: _a new sofa for the living room_____

1. _____

2. _____

3. _____

4. _____

10 Label the furniture on the website.

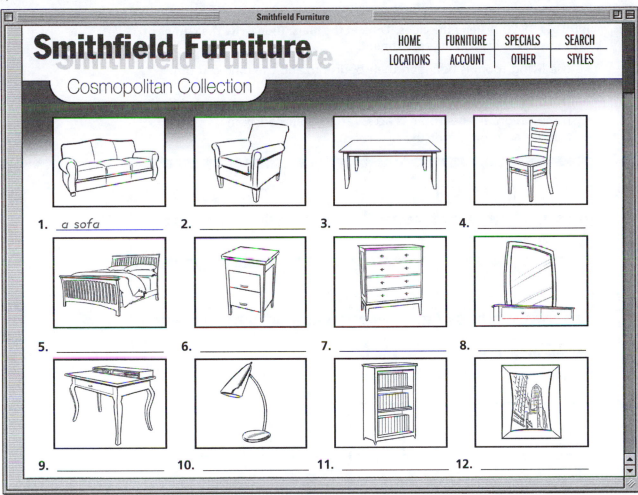

Smithfield Furniture

Smithfield Furniture

HOME | FURNITURE | SPECIALS | SEARCH
LOCATIONS | ACCOUNT | OTHER | STYLES

Cosmopolitan Collection

1. _a sofa_

2. _____

3. _____

4. _____

5. _____

6. _____

7. _____

8. _____

9. _____

10. _____

11. _____

12. _____

11 Complete the conversation. Give your opinion about the furniture in Exercise 10.

1. "Look at that desk. I think it's great! What do you think?"

   YOU _____.

2. "I really like the dresser, too. What do you think?"

   YOU _____.

3. "And what about the bed?"

   YOU _____.

4. "Look at that picture. Do you think it's nice?"

   YOU _____.

12 Describe one room in your home.

A RIDDLE FOR YOU! **Read the clues. Look at the map. Then write the names of
the rooms in Paul and Paula's apartment.**

- The living room is between their bedroom and the dining room.
- The bathroom is across from the living room.
- The kitchen is next to the bathroom, on the left.
- Their daughter's bedroom is across from their bedroom.
- The dining room is not the first room.

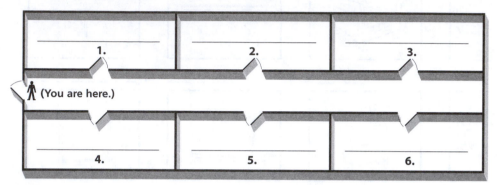

  Complete the puzzle.

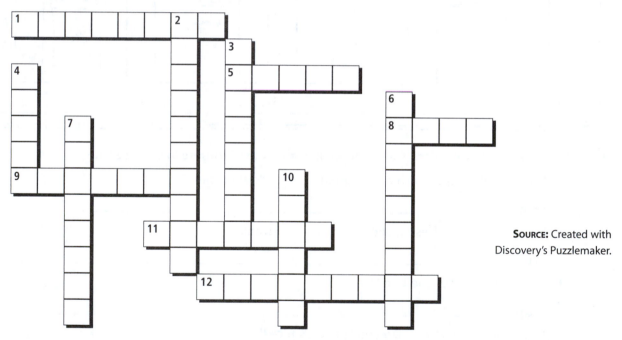

SOURCE: Created with
Discovery's Puzzlemaker.

Across

1. A place where doctors and nurses work
5. It's on the first floor of an office building.
8. Not beautiful
9. The room where the freezer is
11. The room where the night table is
12. In the dining room, there are a table,
chairs, and a _____.

Down

2. A refrigerator, a stove, and a TV are all ____.
3. My office is on the thirty-second floor. Take
the _____.
4. Look at this lamp. What do you _____?
6. A bed, an easy chair, and a desk are all ____.
7. The room where the shower is
10. A place for your clothes

Riddle: 1. daughter's bedroom; 2. bathroom; 3. kitchen; 4. Paul and Paula's bedroom; 5. living room; 6. dining room

CHECKPOINT

 Circle the word that is different.

1. athlete	classmate	neighbor	colleague
2. nurse	engineer	factory	scientist
3. last name	mall	address	phone number
4. hospital	train station	museum	boss
5. brother	daughter	wife	grandmother
6. tall	new	handsome	young
7. speech	party	restaurant	play
8. skirt	blouse	dress	tie
9. lobby	elevator	office	bedroom
10. shower	stove	toilet	bathtub

 Read the ad for an event.

Women's Soccer
Russia and Brazil

Crane Stadium
Saturday, May 15th
1:00 P.M.

Tickets on sale now!
www.sportstix.com

Now write a question for each answer.

1. A: _____?

   B: A soccer game.

2. A: _____?

   B: At Crane Stadium.

3. A: _____?

   B: At one o'clock.

4. A: _____?

   B: On Saturday, May 15th.

3 Read about Salma Hayek.

This is Salma Hayek. She's an actor. She's from Mexico. Her last name, Hayek, is Lebanese. Her father's family is from Lebanon. Her mother is Mexican. Her father is a businessman, and her mother is an opera singer. She has one brother. His name is Sami Hayek. He's a furniture designer. Salma Hayek's birthday is September 2, 1966. She's a Virgo. Hayek is short and very pretty. She lives in a three-bedroom house in Los Angeles, California.

Hayek's 2002 movie *Frida* is about the famous Mexican artist Frida Kahlo. Hayek is Frida in the movie. Alfred Molina is her husband, the artist Diego Rivera. Lots of Hayek's friends are also in the movie.

The colors, art, and music in this movie are beautiful. The movie, the artists, and the actors are great. Already a classic!

Source: Adapted from www.stelladesigns.com.

Now answer the questions.

1. What does Salma Hayek do? _____.

2. Is she from Lebanon? _____.

3. Does Hayek have brothers and sisters? _____.

4. When is her birthday? _____.

5. How old is she? _____.

6. Is she tall? _____.

7. Where does she live? _____.

8. What's her house like? _____.

4 Compare Frida Kahlo and Salma Hayek. Complete the chart. Use the reading in Exercise 3.

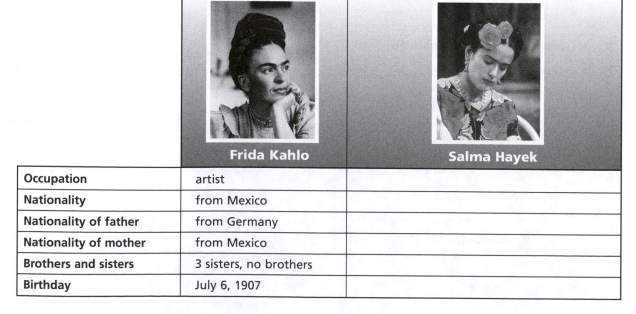

	Frida Kahlo	Salma Hayek
Occupation	artist	
Nationality	from Mexico	
Nationality of father	from Germany	
Nationality of mother	from Mexico	
Brothers and sisters	3 sisters, no brothers	
Birthday	July 6, 1907	

5 Choose one family member, friend, neighbor, or colleague. Complete the information.

1. Name: _____

2. Relationship to you: _____

3. Occupation: _____

4. Brothers and sisters: _____

5. Birthday, Age (How old?), Sign: _____

6. Adjectives to describe the person: _____

7. Likes (places, events, clothes): _____

8. Description of home (What's it like?): _____

Now write about this person. Use the information above.

OPTIONAL VOCABULARY BOOSTER ACTIVITIES

1 Write the article.

1. _____ florist

2. _____ accountant

3. _____ hairdresser

4. _____ reporter

5. _____ electrician

6. _____ dentist

2 Who works in these places? Write an occupation for each place. Use **a** or **an**.

1. a travel agency: _____

2. a bank: _____

3. a restaurant: _____

4. an office: _____

5. a pharmacy: _____

6. a supermarket: _____

7. a department store: _____

8. a gas station: _____

Describe the locations of the places.

Example: your dry cleaners: *It's on Flowers Street, around the corner from the police station*.

1. your supermarket: _____

_____.

2. your video store or fire station: _____

_____.

3. your favorite clothing store or electronics store: _____

_____.

4 **Which events do you like? Number the events from 1 to 8 in the order you like them.**

____ movies

____ ballets

____ operas

____ concerts

____ art exhibitions

____ baseball games

____ volleyball games

____ football games

5 **Check** ☑ **the items you have in your home. Then write which room they are in.**

1. ☐ an intercom _____

2. ☐ a fire escape _____

3. ☐ a medicine cabinet _____

4. ☐ a shower curtain _____

5. ☐ a dishwasher _____

6. ☐ a coffee maker _____

7. ☐ a food processor _____

8. ☐ a fax machine _____

6 Write <u>this</u>, <u>that</u>, <u>these</u>, or <u>those</u> and the name of the clothes.

Do you like _____?
1.

I need
_____, but I
2.
want _____.
3.

Are _____
4.
black or blue?

Look at
_____.
5.
They're really nice.

7 Go shopping for your home. What colors do you want? Write sentences.
Use an article with singular nouns.

Example: sheets: *I want gray sheets*_____.

1. blanket: _____.

2. napkins: _____.

3. bath mat: _____.

4. towels: _____.

5. place mats: _____.

6. plates: _____.

Activities

LESSON 1

1 **YOUR MORNING ACTIVITIES.** Put the activities in order. Write ordinal numbers (1st, 2nd, . . .) on the lines. Write an <u>X</u> next to the activities you don't do.

_____ take a shower / a bath

_____ eat breakfast

_____ put on my makeup

_____ get up

_____ shave

_____ get dressed

_____ brush my teeth

_____ comb / brush my hair

Choose your first three morning activities. What time do you do them?

1. _____.

2. _____.

3. _____.

2 **Write the room where you do each activity.**

1. take a shower / a bath: _in the bathroom_____

2. get dressed: _____

3. comb / brush my hair: _____

4. eat dinner: _____

5. watch TV: _____

6. study: _____

3 **Look at the activities and the times. Write sentences in the simple present tense.**

1. _She comes home at 6:30_____.   2. _____.

3. _____.   4. _____.

4 ▸ **Write the name of a family member or friend. Check ☑ his or her activities.**

Name: _____

☐ takes a shower in the evening   ☐ studies after dinner
☐ takes a shower in the morning   ☐ watches TV after dinner
☐ doesn't eat breakfast   ☐ gets up early on the weekend
☐ eats a big breakfast   ☐ gets up late on the weekend

Now write sentences about this person.

_____
_____
_____
_____

5 ▸ **Complete the conversation.**

Are you a morning person or an evening person?

1. YOU _____ .

Why do you say that?

2. YOU _____ .

LESSON 2

6 ▸ **Look at the pictures. Then write sentences about the household chores Mr. and Mrs. Rand do.**

Mr. Rand

1. _Mr. Rand washes the dishes_ .

2. _____ .

3. _____ .

Mrs. Rand

4. _____ .

5. _____ .

6. _____ .

7 Look at Lawrence's weekly schedule.

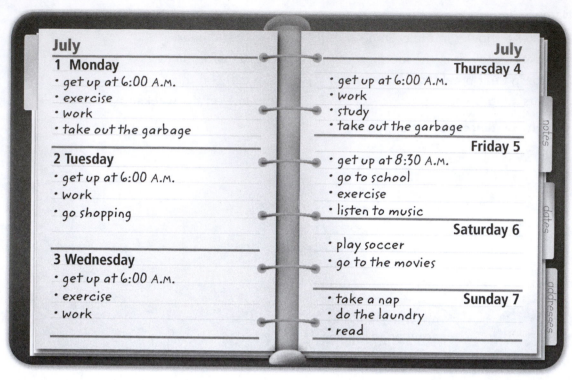

July

1 Monday
- get up at 6:00 A.M.
- exercise
- work
- take out the garbage

2 Tuesday
- get up at 6:00 A.M.
- work
- go shopping

3 Wednesday
- get up at 6:00 A.M.
- exercise
- work

July

Thursday 4
- get up at 6:00 A.M.
- work
- study
- take out the garbage

Friday 5
- get up at 8:30 A.M.
- go to school
- exercise
- listen to music

Saturday 6
- play soccer
- go to the movies

Sunday 7
- take a nap
- do the laundry
- read

notes · dates · addresses

Now complete the sentences about Lawrence.

1. Lawrence _____ once a week.

2. He _____ twice a week.

3. He _____ three times a week.

4. He _____ four days a week.

5. On Fridays, he _____.

6. On Friday evenings, he _____.

7. On the weekend, he _____.

 8 Look at Lawrence's weekly schedule again. Complete the conversation between Alicia and Lawrence.

1. **Alicia:** What's your typical week like?

   Lawrence: _____.

2. **Alicia:** And what about Fridays?

   Lawrence: _____.

3. **Alicia:** What do you do on the weekend?

   Lawrence: _____.

4. **Alicia:** Sounds like you're pretty busy. When do you do your chores?

   Lawrence: _____.

LESSON 3

9 **How often do you . . . ? Check ✔ always, usually, sometimes, or never.**

	always	usually	sometimes	never
1. eat breakfast	☐	☐	☐	☐
2. watch TV in the evening	☐	☐	☐	☐
3. go to bed before 11:00 P.M.	☐	☐	☐	☐
4. take a bath	☐	☐	☐	☐
5. read before bed	☐	☐	☐	☐
6. exercise in the morning	☐	☐	☐	☐
7. make the bed	☐	☐	☐	☐
8. wash the dishes after dinner	☐	☐	☐	☐
9. listen to music at home	☐	☐	☐	☐
10. take a nap	☐	☐	☐	☐

10 **WHAT ABOUT YOU? Answer the questions.**

1. What do you do every day? _____.

2. What do you do twice a day? _____.

3. Where do you usually eat lunch? _____.

4. What do you usually do after dinner on weekdays? _____.

5. What do you do about once a week? _____.

6. What do you do on Friday nights? _____.

11 **Write sentences about the daily activities or weekly schedule of a family member or a friend.**

Example: *My brother always goes to the movies on Fridays.* _____

_____

_____

_____

_____

A RIDDLE FOR YOU!

What comes once in an afternoon, twice in a week, but never in a day or a month?
(Hint: It comes once in the alphabet.)

Answer: _____

 WORD FIND. Look across (→) and down (↓). Circle the seven household chores or work activities and the seven leisure activities. Then write the chores / work activities and leisure activities on the lines.

```
W  A  T  C  H  T  V  U  C  E  A  K  A  U  H  I  T
E  P  N  A  C  O  H  C  L  H  S  O  I  K  V  R  I
K  L  W  A  S  H  T  H  E  D  I  S  H  E  S  E  A
G  A  L  M  S  G  A  N  A  M  C  T  M  N  M  A  M
E  Y  L  M  G  O  A  L  N  K  B  A  O  H  A  D  K
T  S  O  R  O  D  T  N  T  S  D  K  W  W  K  W  O
V  O  A  G  T  A  A  T  H  A  A  E  T  N  E  V  O
A  C  E  D  O  N  S  C  E  U  N  A  H  I  D  A  I
C  C  S  A  W  C  Y  H  H  O  M  B  E  A  I  W  I
U  E  N  U  O  I  C  S  O  E  U  A  L  O  N  H  E
U  R  S  R  R  N  B  T  U  T  E  T  A  D  N  S  E
M  L  N  S  K  G  E  G  S  O  O  H  W  A  E  A  E
C  H  C  B  D  O  T  H  E  L  A  U  N  D  R  Y  D
T  E  L  I  S  T  E  N  T  O  M  U  S  I  C  H  D
T  E  T  A  K  E  A  N  A  P  E  N  H  A  O  I  E
L  H  T  I  A  K  N  T  T  U  E  W  W  N  S  S  A
```

SOURCE: Created with www.spellbuilder.com.

Chores / Work Activities	Leisure Activities
_____	_____
_____	_____
_____	_____
_____	_____
_____	_____
_____	_____
_____	_____

Riddle: the letter g

Weather and Ongoing Activities

LESSON 1

 What's the weather like? Is it hot, cold, warm, or cool?

1. _____

2. _____

3. _____

4. _____

 Look at the pictures. What are the people doing right now? Write sentences in the present continuous.

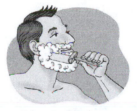

1. _She's brushing her teeth_____.

2. _____.

3. _____.

4. _____.

5. _____.

6. _____.

3 Look at the pictures. Answer the questions. Use a short answer and the present continuous.

1. Is he taking a bath? *No, he isn't. He's taking a shower.*

2. Is she reading? _____

3. Are they listening to music? _____

4. Is she wearing a dress? _____

5. Is it snowing? _____

4 Where's Andrea? What's she doing? Match the places with Andrea's activities.

1. _____ She's in the kitchen.
2. _____ She's in the bedroom.
3. _____ She's in the bathroom.
4. _____ She's in the dining room.
5. _____ She's in the office.
6. _____ She's in the living room.

a. She's going to bed.
b. She's checking her e-mail.
c. She's eating dinner with her family.
d. She's reading in the easy chair.
e. She's brushing her teeth.
f. She's making breakfast.

LESSON 2

5 Look at the Ryan family's living room. Then read the answers and write questions about the family's activities. Use the present continuous.

1. **A:** *Where's the grandfather taking a nap* _____ ? **B:** On the sofa.

2. **A:** _____ ? **B:** Washing the dishes.

3. **A:** _____ ? **B:** They're going to a concert.

4. **A:** _____ ? **B:** The son is.

5. **A:** _____ ? **B:** An apple.

6. **A:** _____ ? **B:** Playing.

6 Imagine a really great day. Answer the questions in complete sentences.

1. Where are you? _____.

2. Who's there? _____.

3. What are you doing? _____.

4. What's the weather like? _____.

5. What are you wearing? _____.

7 Write the present participles.

1. take _____ 6. do _____

2. play _____ 7. drive _____

3. study _____ 8. call _____

4. exercise _____ 9. go _____

5. eat _____ 10. get dressed _____

LESSON 3

8 ▷ **Write the time, date, month, or year.**

1. right now: _____

2. today: _____

3. tomorrow: _____

4. the day after tomorrow: _____

5. this month: _____

6. this year: _____

9 ▷ **WHAT ABOUT YOU? Answer the questions in the present continuous.**

1. What are you doing today? _____.

2. What are you doing tonight? _____.

3. What are you doing tomorrow? _____.

4. What are you doing tomorrow evening? _____.

5. What are you doing this weekend? _____.

10 ▷ **Respond to the instant messages with your <u>own</u> information. Create your <u>own</u> screen name.**

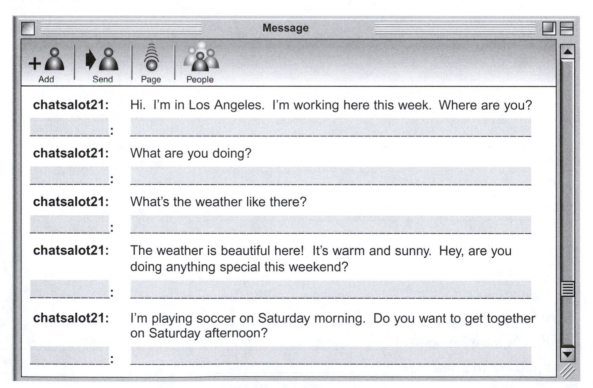

	Message
chatsalot21:	Hi. I'm in Los Angeles. I'm working here this week. Where are you?
_____:	_____
chatsalot21:	What are you doing?
_____:	_____
chatsalot21:	What's the weather like there?
_____:	_____
chatsalot21:	The weather is beautiful here! It's warm and sunny. Hey, are you doing anything special this weekend?
_____:	_____
chatsalot21:	I'm playing soccer on Saturday morning. Do you want to get together on Saturday afternoon?
_____:	_____

11 ▷ **Write your plans for next week. Write sentences in the present continuous.**

1 ▷ **Complete the puzzle. First, unscramble the letters of the time expressions. Then write the letters in the numbered boxes in the other boxes with the same number.**

Time expressions

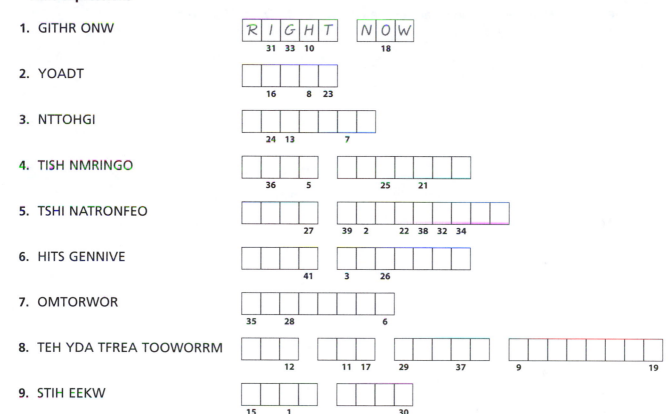

1. GITHR ONW — R I G H T | N O W
   31 33 10 / 18

2. YOADT
   16 8 23

3. NTTOHGI
   24 13   7

4. TISH NMRINGO
   36 5 / 25 21

5. TSHI NATRONFEO
   27 / 39 2   22 38 32 34

6. HITS GENNIVE
   41 3   26

7. OMTORWOR
   35 28   6

8. TEH YDA TFREA TOOWORRM
   12 / 11 17 / 29 37 / 9   19

9. STIH EEKW
   15 1 / 30

10. TISH MOTHN
    4 14 / 40 20

Puzzle

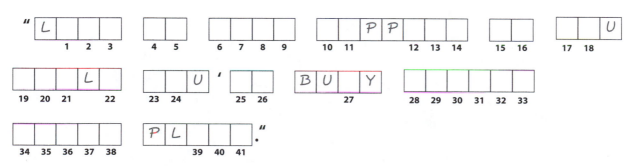

" L _ _ _ _ _ _ _ _ _ _ P P _ _ _ _ _ _ U
  1 2 3 4 5 6 7 8 9 10 11 12 13 14 15 16 17 18

_ _ L _ _ _ U ' _ _ B U _ Y _ _ _ _ _ _
19 20 21 22 23 24 25 26 27 28 29 30 31 32 33

_ _ _ _ _ P L _ _ _ . "
34 35 36 37 38 39 40 41

—John Lennon, singer and musician (U.K.)

SOURCE: Created with Discovery's Puzzlemaker.

TAKE A GUESS! **Match the weather and the places.**

1. _____ Number 1 hot place in the world
2. _____ Number 1 cold place in the world
3. _____ Number 1 rainy place in the world
4. _____ Number 1 snowy place in the world
5. _____ Number 1 sunny place in the world
6. _____ Number 1 cloudy place in the world

a. Plateau Station, Antarctica
b. Eastern Sahara Desert, Africa
c. Ben Nevis, Scotland
d. Mount Baker, Washington, U.S.A.
e. Cherrapunji, India
f. Dallol, Ethiopia

Guess: 1. f; 2. a; 3. e; 4. d; 5. b; 6. c

Food

LESSON 1

1 ⟩ **Complete the chart. Check ✔ the boxes.**

	oranges	bananas	eggs	tomatoes	apples	lemons	peas	peppers	potatoes	beans	onions
I like											
I don't like											
I have in my kitchen											
I need											
I eat every day											
I sometimes eat											
I never eat											

2 ⟩ **Look at the recipe.**

Vegetable Omelet

Ingredients:

3 potatoes

6 eggs

1 small tomato

1/2 an onion

1/2 a pepper

Now answer the questions.

1. Are there any potatoes in the omelet? _____.

2. How many eggs are there? _____.

3. Are there any onions? _____.

4. How many tomatoes are there in the omelet? _____.

5. Which ingredients do <u>you</u> have for this recipe? _____.

6. Which ingredients do <u>you</u> need? _____.

3 ⟩ **Write questions with How many. Then answer the questions.**

1. students / your English class: _How many students are there in your English class_ ?
   _____ .

2. people / your family: _____ ?
   _____ .

3. days / this month: _____ ?
   _____ .

4. sweaters / your closet: _____ ?
   _____ .

5. bathrooms / your home: _____ ?
   _____ .

LESSON 2

4 ⟩ **Count or non-count? Write a, an, or X before each food or drink.**

1. _____ tea   5. _____ egg   9. _____ cheese
2. _____ rice   6. _____ sugar   10. _____ lemon
3. _____ banana   7. _____ oil   11. _____ juice
4. _____ meat   8. _____ apple   12. _____ onion

5 ⟩ **Do you keep these foods in the fridge? On the shelf? On the counter?
Write four sentences.**

I keep soup, pasta, and
sugar on the shelf.

juice	bread	milk
rice	butter	eggs
oil	tomatoes	tea

1. _____ .
2. _____ .
3. _____ .
4. _____ .

6 ⟩ **What color is it? What color are they? Write sentences.**

1. milk: _Milk is white_ _____ .
2. eggs: _____ .
3. butter: _____ .
4. orange juice: _____ .
5. tomatoes: _____ .
6. coffee: _____ .

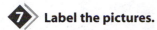

7 **Label the pictures.**

1. _a loaf of bread_

2. _____

3. _____

4. _____

5. _____

8 **Write five sentences. Use words or phrases from each box.**

How many How much Is there any Are there any	+	meat juice oranges sugar bananas onions bread cans of soup	+	in the fridge? are there on the counter? do we have? is there? on the shelf? do you want? are there? in the kitchen?

1. _Are there any oranges in the fridge?_ _____

2. _____

3. _____

4. _____

5. _____

6. _____

9 **Look at the picture.**

Complete the questions with <u>How much</u> or <u>How many</u>. Then answer the questions.

1. A: _____ peppers are there?   B: _____ .

2. A: _____ water is in the fridge?   B: _____ .

3. A: _____ bags of beans are there?   B: _____ .

4. A: _____ soda is there?   B: _____ .

10 **Look at the picture in Exercise 9 again. Complete the questions with <u>Are there any</u> or <u>Is there any</u>. Then answer the questions.**

1. A: _____ cheese in the fridge?   B: _____ .

2. A: _____ eggs?   B: _____ .

3. A: _____ juice?   B: _____ .

4. A: _____ butter?   B: _____ .

11 **What's for dinner? Answer the questions in a restaurant.**

1. "Would you like tomato soup or onion soup?"

   YOU _____ .

2. "And would you like chicken or meat?"

   YOU _____ .

3. "Would you like potatoes or brown rice?"

   YOU _____ .

4. "Would you like coffee or tea later?"

   YOU _____ .

5. "And then would you like an apple or an orange?"

   YOU _____ .

LESSON 3

12 **Complete each sentence. Circle the letter.**

1. Dr. Roberts _____ his e-mail every day.

   a. check   **b.** checks   **c.** is checking

2. Theresa _____ the laundry on Mondays.

   a. do   **b.** does   **c.** is doing

3. Lucas and Nate aren't at home. They _____ soccer in the park.

   a. play   **b.** plays   **c.** are playing

4. I _____ chicken with peppers for dinner. Would you like to join me?

   a. make   **b.** makes   **c.** am making

5. Mr. and Mrs. Juster usually _____ meat.

   a. doesn't eat   **b.** don't eat   **c.** aren't eating

13 **Complete the conversations. Use the simple present tense or the present continuous.**

1. **A:** What _____ right now?
   <u>you / eat</u>

   B: Chicken soup.

2. **A:** _____ milk in his coffee?
   <u>he / want</u>

   B: No, he doesn't. But he would like sugar.

3. **A:** What _____ in the fridge?
   <u>we / have</u>

   B: Soda, cheese, and an apple.

4. **A:** I _____ a dress to the party on Friday. How about you?
   <u>wear</u>

   B: I never _____ dresses.
   <u>wear</u>

5. **A:** _____ on Saturdays?
   <u>Jeff / work</u>

   B: Yes, usually. But this Saturday he _____ soccer.
   <u>play</u>

6. **A:** Where _____ lunch on Tuesdays?
   <u>you / eat</u>

   B: At Eli's Café. But today we _____ to City Bistro for my boss's birthday.
   <u>go</u>

JUST FOR FUN

 A RIDDLE FOR YOU!

George, Helen, and Steve are drinking coffee. Bart, Karen, and Dave are drinking soda.
Is Ellie drinking coffee or soda?
(Hint: Look at the letters in each drink.)

Answer: _____

SOURCE: able2know.com.

 Complete the puzzle.

Across

2. A _____ of bread

4. Salt and _____

5. In Asia, people eat a lot of _____.

8. Directions for cooking something

10. You make this drink with lemons, water, and sugar.

11. A box, a bottle, a bag, and a can are all _____.

13. I like coffee with milk and _____.

Down

1. The place for milk: ____ ____

3. Would you like apple juice, _____ juice, or tomato juice?

6. The foods in a recipe

7. Water, tea, and soda are all _____.

9. In the omelet, there are three _____.

12. Peppers, peas, and _____ are green.

SOURCE: Created with Discovery's Puzzlemaker.

Riddle: Ellie is drinking coffee.

UNIT 11

Past Events

LESSON 1

1 ▷ **Write the date, month, or year.**

1. yesterday: _____
2. last Wednesday: _____
3. three days ago: _____
4. one week ago: _____

5. last month: _____
6. two months ago: _____
7. last year: _____
8. five years ago: _____

2 ▷ **Complete the questions with <u>was</u> or <u>were</u>. Then answer the questions.**

1. Where _*were*_ you last night at 9:00? *I was at home* _____.
2. _____ you at school yesterday? _____.
3. How _____ the weather last week? _____.
4. _____ there milk in your refrigerator this morning? _____.
5. What _____ your first e-mail address? _____.
6. When _____ your birthday? _____.
7. How old _____ you in 1996? _____.
8. Who _____ your favorite singer in the nineties? _____.

LESSON 2

3 ▷ **Complete the paragraph. Use the simple past tense forms of the verbs in the box. Use each verb only once.**

be	eat	put	wake
come	get	see	not exercise
drive	go	take	not read

Amy _____ home late last night. She and her colleagues _____ a movie after work.
    1.   **2.**

After the movie, they _____ out for dinner. This morning Amy _____ up at 8:00.
                            3.   **4.**

She usually wakes up at 7:00. She _____ a shower and _____ dressed by 8:10.
                                        5.   **6.**

She usually takes the bus to work, but today she _____. In the car, she _____
                                              7.   **8.**

on her makeup and _____ a banana for breakfast. She _____, and she _____
                      9.   **10.**   **11.**

the newspaper. But Amy _____ only five minutes late to work.
                      12.

4 **Write five sentences about your activities this morning. Look at the pictures for ideas.**

_____
_____
_____
_____
_____
_____
_____

5 **Which activities do you like? Number the activities from 1 to 6 in the order you like to do them.**

_____ go to the beach

_____ go swimming

_____ go for a walk

_____ go running

_____ go bike riding

_____ go for a drive

Which activity did you do? Which activity didn't you do? Write three sentences about <u>yesterday</u>, <u>last week</u>, and <u>last month</u>.

Examples: _I went to the beach yesterday_____ .

_I didn't go bike riding last week_____ .

1. _____ .

2. _____ .

3. _____ .

6 Write three things you did last weekend. Write three things you **didn't** do.

What I did

1. _____.

2. _____.

3. _____.

What I didn't do

4. _____.

5. _____.

6. _____.

LESSON 3

7 Circle the seasons where you live. Then write the months in each season where you live.

spring: _____

summer: _____

fall: _____

winter: _____

8 What's the weather usually like? Write the seasons where you live. Then check ✔ the weather where you live.

Seasons	cloudy	windy	sunny	cold	hot	warm	cool

9 **WHAT ABOUT YOU?** **Answer the questions.**

1. Did you eat breakfast this morning? _____.

2. Where did you eat lunch yesterday? _____.

3. How many books did you read last month? _____.

4. Where did you live five years ago? _____.

5. What time did you come home last night? _____.

6. Did you go to any movies last month? What did you see? _____

_____.

7. How often did you watch TV last week? _____.

8. What did you do last summer? _____.

10 **Read the postcard from Luke's vacation.**

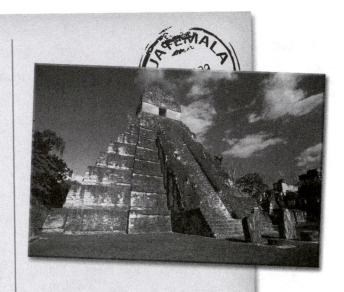

Hello from Guatemala!

I'm in Antigua, Guatemala. I'm studying
Spanish. I go to class every morning, and
every afternoon there's an activity. On
Monday, we rode bikes to a coffee farm.
On Tuesday, there was a Latin dance
class. On Wednesday, we took a bus to
Chichicastenango and shopped in the
market. Yesterday we went to a
Guatemalan restaurant for lunch. Now
I'm in the ancient Mayan city of Tikal
for the weekend. It's beautiful.
Thinking of you!

Luke

Now look at the answers and write questions in the simple past tense.

1. A: _____? **B:** To Guatemala.

2. A: _____? **B:** He studied Spanish.

3. A: _____? **B:** Every morning.

4. A: _____? **B:** On Tuesday.

5. A: _____? **B:** He took a bus.

6. A: _____? **B:** In a restaurant.

11 Write a postcard about your last vacation. **Answer five or more questions in the box.**

When was it?	Where did you go?
What did you see?	What did you do?
What did you really like?	What did you <u>not</u> like?
How was the weather?	What did you eat?

Dear _____,

_____

_____

_____

_____

_____

_____

12 Choose the correct words to complete the conversation. Write the letter on the line.

1. **A:** Hi, how's it going?

   B: _____

2. **A:** I was on vacation. I just got back yesterday.

   B: _____

3. **A:** I went to Hawaii for ten days.

   B: _____

4. **A:** Really nice.

   B: _____

5. **A:** I went to the beach every day. I went swimming and snorkeling. And I went sightseeing.

   B: _____

   A: Thanks!

a. What did you do?

b. Where did you go?

c. Pretty good. Hey, where were you last week?

d. Sounds wonderful. It's great to see you. Welcome back.

e. How was it?

JUST FOR FUN

 A RIDDLE FOR YOU!

Where is the only place that yesterday always comes after today?
(Hint: Think of a book.)

Answer: _____

SOURCE: www.didyouknow.cd.

2 **WORD FIND.** **Look across (→) and down (↓). Circle the base forms of the 20 verbs. Then write the simple past tense forms of those verbs on the lines.**

```
H A V E Y E H Y K K E R R T K A E L E
E C G E Y L P K L E N U I A K N T W S
C S E E I E P C C P V I D W W D A R I
T A I A A W A B O H Y E C M T L I L
T O N A T R T D L E C U E H N E K T O
E E W E A R A H I I P A E E T I A E E
L A O T L Y K R S W R D T C W A K E I
V A R N L D E E T O A S A K L O V E I
V T E B H R Y D E T C D R I V E T I I
E Y A L T I P R N T T W E W A I E O V
A N D G R A L D L E I A E I E L K H I
T Y N C A E A K E L C S L M V S E W H
C H E H W E Y A G K E H W A T E C R V
A R K L T A I A E W R E T K I A E E A
C L E A N D W E T I P A E E N G A W R
K S L E I C U A C I P E R W E L R C D
```

SOURCE: Created with www.spellbuilder.com.

_____ _____ _____ _____
_____ _____ _____ _____
_____ _____ _____ _____
_____ _____ _____ _____
_____ _____ _____ _____

Riddle: In a dictionary

Appearance and Health

LESSON 1

1 ▶ Check ☑ the adjectives that describe you.

1. My hair

   ☐ black   ☐ blonde   ☐ straight   ☐ short

   ☐ brown   ☐ gray   ☐ wavy   ☐ long

   ☐ red   ☐ white   ☐ curly   ☐ bald

2. My eyes

   ☐ brown   ☐ blue   ☐ green

2 ▶ Describe a family member, a friend, or a colleague. Fill in the chart.

| Person | Hair | | | Eye color |
	color	straight, wavy, or curly	long, short, or bald	
My brother	blonde	straight	short	blue

3 ▶ Write the parts of the face.

eyebrow	nose
eye	mouth
eyelashes	chin
ear	neck

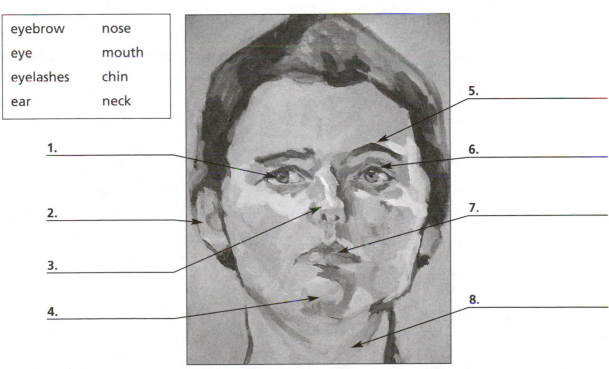

1. _____

2. _____

3. _____

4. _____

5. _____

6. _____

7. _____

8. _____

4 **Look at Exercise 1 again.** Use the information to write sentences with <u>be</u> about yourself.

Example: _My hair is brown_ .

1. _____.

2. _____.

3. _____.

5 **Look at Exercise 2 again.** Use the information to write sentences with <u>have</u> about a family member, a friend, or a colleague.

Example: _My brother has blue eyes_ .

1. _____.

2. _____.

3. _____.

6 **Choose three famous people to describe.**

Here's language you already know:

pretty	short
handsome	tall
good-looking	old
cute	young

1. _Nicole Kidman_ : _She's tall. She's pretty. She has long, curly, red hair._
Her eyes are blue. She's an actress from Australia.
_____
_____

2. _____ : _____
_____
_____
_____

3. _____ : _____
_____
_____
_____

4. _____ : _____
_____
_____
_____

LESSON 2

 Write the parts of the body.

1. _____

2. _____

3. _____

4. _____

5. _____

6. _____

7. _____

8. _____

head	neck	shoulder
chest	arm	hand
hip	leg	knee
ankle	foot	
stomach / abdomen		

9. _____

10. _____

11. _____

12. _____

 What happened? Write a sentence about each picture.

1. _She burned her hand_ _____.

2. _____.

3. _____.

4. _____.

5. _____.

Now complete the conversation.

6. **A:** _____?

   B: I broke my leg.

7. **A:** _____.

   B: Thanks!

LESSON 3

9 Check ✓ the remedies for each ailment.

	take something	lie down	have some tea	see a doctor	see a dentist	don't go to work or school	eat	don't eat
a cold								
a fever								
a sore throat								
a stomachache								
a backache								
a toothache								

10 Think about an ailment you had. Then answer the questions.

> **Be careful:**
>
> Lie is irregular in the simple past tense:
>
> lie (down) ➡ lay (down)

1. What was wrong? _____.

2. What did you do? _____.

11 Your friend Brendan is going out with a colleague tonight. He wants your advice. Answer his questions.

1. **Brendan:** "We're going to the movies. What should we see?"

    YOU _____.

2. **Brendan:** "After the movie, we're going out for dinner. Where should we go?"

    YOU _____.

3. **Brendan:** "Should I talk about work?"

    YOU _____.

4. **Brendan:** "What should I wear?"

    YOU _____.

1 ▷ **Complete the puzzle. First, unscramble the letters of the ailments. Then write the letters in the numbered boxes in other boxes with the same number.**

Ailments

1. ONT ELEF LLEW [N][O][T] [F][E][E][L] [W][E][L][L]
                           17   19   8

2. A ODLC [ ] [ ][ ][ ][ ]
                  4

3. A UOCHG [ ] [ ][ ][ ][ ]
                7

4. A RESO OTARHT [ ] [ ][ ][ ][ ] [ ][ ][ ][ ][ ]
                  10   13

5. A SOACHHCAETM [ ] [ ][ ][ ][ ][ ][ ][ ][ ][ ]
                                 15

6. A EEVFR [ ] [ ][ ][ ][ ]
              1   14

7. A AADEECHH [ ] [ ][ ][ ][ ][ ][ ][ ]
                 9   6

8. NA REAHEAC [ ][ ] [ ][ ][ ][ ][ ]
              3   16

9. A KCABEACH [ ] [ ][ ][ ][ ][ ][ ][ ]
             12   18

10. A OOTTHCHEA [ ] [ ][ ][ ][ ][ ][ ][ ]
              11   5

11. A YNURN SEON [ ] [ ][ ][ ][ ] [ ][ ][ ]
              20   2

Puzzle

" [ ][ ][ ][ ] [ ] [ ][ ][ ][ ] , [ ][ ][ ][ ][ ][ ] [ ] [ ][V][ ] . "
   1 2 3 4   5   6 7 8 9   10 11 12 13 14 15 16 17 18 19 20

—An old saying

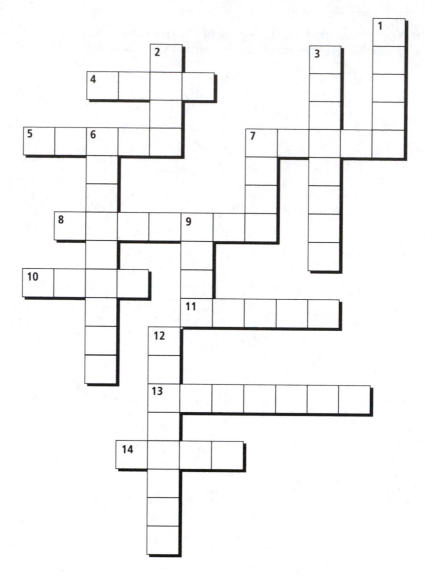

Across

4. It's between your hip and your ankle.
5. Hair on a man's chin
7. They're white. They're in your mouth.
8. They're on your hands. You have ten.
10. Parts of the body for shoes
11. Not long
13. Another word for "abdomen"
14. Doesn't have hair

Down

1. It's between your nose and your chin.
2. Part of the body for a hat
3. Take something, lie down, and have some tea are all ____.
6. Burn your finger, cut your hand, and fall down are all ____.
7. They're on your feet. You have ten.
9. What you use to see
12. Hair between a man's nose and mouth

Source: Created with Discovery's Puzzlemaker.

Abilities and Requests

LESSON 1

1 Complete the chart. Check ☑ your abilities and skills.

	play the violin	play the piano	drive a car	speak English	cook fish	make onion soup	play soccer
I can . . .							
I can't . . .							

2 Complete the conversations with <u>can</u> or <u>can't</u> and the base form of a verb.

1. **A:** _____ you _____ English?

   B: Oh, yes, and I _____ _____ Spanish, too.

2. **A:** _____ you _____ my computer?

   B: Fix it? No. I _____ _____ cars but not computers.

3. **A:** _____ you _____ my picture?

   B: No. I'm an engineer, not an artist.

4. **A:** _____ you _____ a sweater for me?

   B: Sorry. I can sew, but I _____ _____.

5. **A:** _____ you _____ the violin?

   B: No, but I _____ _____ the guitar.

3 Write about four different people. Complete the sentences with <u>can</u> or <u>can't</u> and an ability or skill.

Example: My sister: _Anna can fix a car_____.

1. My teacher: _____.

2. My friend: _____.

3. My neighbor: _____.

4. My colleague: _____.

Which occupation is good for you? Take the *Top Notch* Skills and Interests Survey.

Top Notch Skills and Interests Survey

SKILLS

		Do very well	Do well	Do OK	Do poorly	Can't do
1.	paint	◯	◯	◯	◯	◯
2.	draw	◯	◯	◯	◯	◯
3.	dance	◯	◯	◯	◯	◯
4.	swim	◯	◯	◯	◯	◯
5.	drive	◯	◯	◯	◯	◯
6.	play the violin	◯	◯	◯	◯	◯
7.	ski	◯	◯	◯	◯	◯
8.	fix a car	◯	◯	◯	◯	◯
9.	cook	◯	◯	◯	◯	◯
10.	sing	◯	◯	◯	◯	◯

INTERESTS

		Like a lot	Like	Like a little	Don't like
1.	go to concerts	◯	◯	◯	◯
2.	go to museums	◯	◯	◯	◯
3.	listen to music	◯	◯	◯	◯
4.	make dinner for friends	◯	◯	◯	◯
5.	exercise	◯	◯	◯	◯
6.	go running	◯	◯	◯	◯
7.	go bike riding	◯	◯	◯	◯
8.	go for a drive	◯	◯	◯	◯

RESULTS

Look at your answers.
What do you do very well? What do you like to do a lot?

Can you cook well? Do you like to make dinner for friends?	➡	Maybe you should be a chef.
Can you sing, dance, play the violin (guitar, piano, other instruments)? Do you like to go to concerts and listen to music?	➡	Maybe you should be a singer or musician.
Can you swim and ski? Do you like to exercise and go running and bike riding?	➡	Maybe you should be an athlete.
Can you draw and paint? Do you like to go to museums?	➡	Maybe you should be an artist.
Can you drive and fix a car? Do you like to go for a drive?	➡	Maybe you should be a mechanic.

According to the survey, what should you be? _____

Answer the questions.

What can you do?

When did you learn?

Example: *I can knit* .

1. _____ .

3. _____ .

5. _____ .

Example: *About two years ago* .

2. _____ .

4. _____ .

6. _____ .

LESSON 2

 Write sentences with <u>too</u> and an adjective.

1. She can't drive.

   She's too young .

2. She can't watch TV.

   _____ .

3. You can't wear that shirt.

   _____ .

4. He doesn't want that suit.

   _____ .

5. We can't go bike riding today.

   _____ .

6. She can't drink this coffee.

   _____ .

7 **Your friend wants to get together, but you decline the invitations. Give reasons.**

1. "Let's go for a drive."

 YOU _____.

2. "OK, let's go out for lunch."

YOU _____.

3. "How about a movie?"

YOU _____.

4. "Well, maybe some other time."

 YOU _____.

LESSON 3

8 **Match the problems with the requests. Write the letter on the line.**

1. _____ I'm cold.
2. _____ I need to check my e-mail.
3. _____ It's too hot.
4. _____ I don't have any clean clothes.
5. _____ I can't read this.
6. _____ There isn't any milk.

a. Could you please do the laundry?
b. Could you please close the window?
c. Could you please turn on the computer?
d. Could you please go shopping?
e. Could you please open the window?
f. Could you please hand me my glasses?

9 **Mrs. Cole's boss is coming for dinner at 6:00. But look at the house!**

Help Mrs. Cole ask her husband to help. Write polite requests with <u>could</u> or <u>can</u>.

1. _Could you please take out the garbage_ _____?
2. _____?
3. _____?
4. _____?
5. _____?

Choose the correct response. Circle the letter.

1. Can you sing?
   a. No, I can't. I sing terribly.   b. Not right now. I'm too busy.   c. No, thanks.

2. When did you learn to ski?
   a. I just got back.   b. The day after tomorrow.   c. Last winter.

3. Let's go shopping.
   a. I'm sorry to hear that.   b. I'm sorry. I have other plans.   c. That's too bad.

4. Could you do me a favor?
   a. Sure. What?   b. Was it hard?   c. How was it?

5. Could you please turn off the TV?
   a. Not at all.   b. Sure. No problem.   c. Maybe some other time.

 Answer the questions. Write about your abilities and skills.

- What can you do well?
- When did you learn?
- What do you do poorly?

1 What can they do? Match the famous people with their abilities.

Mikhail Baryshnikov

Michael Schumacher

1. _____ Daniela Mercury   a. He can write.
2. _____ Adriana Fernandez   b. He can dance.
3. _____ Gabriel Garcia Marquez   c. She can sing.
4. _____ Mikhail Baryshnikov   d. He can drive.
5. _____ Madhur Jaffrey   e. She can play tennis.
6. _____ Serena Williams   f. She can cook.
7. _____ Michael Schumacher   g. She can run.

2 Complete the puzzle.

Across

1. I'm going to bed. Could you please
   _____ _____ the light?

4. Make dinner

6. Not well

7. Luis Miguel can do this.

8. Speak a second language, play the violin,
   and knit are all _____.

10. I'm cold. Could you please _____
    _____ my sweater?

Down

2. A baby can do this at three months.

3. You can do this when there's snow.

5. The shoes are size 35. She wears a 37.
   They're _____ _____.

8. Make clothes

9. You can do this at the beach.

Source: Created with Discovery's Puzzlemaker.

Past, Present, and Future Plans

LESSON 1

1 **Read about Yao Ming's life.**

Yao Ming's Life Story

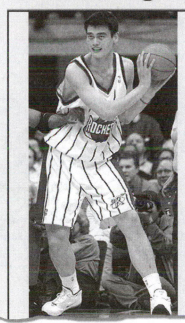

Yao Ming was born on September 12, 1980. He grew up in a small apartment in Shanghai, China, with his parents. They were both basketball players too—and tall! Their son is 2.26 meters (7 feet 5 inches). Yao doesn't have any brothers or sisters. When he was about nine, he went to the Youth Sports School in Shanghai. In China, he played for the Shanghai Sharks.

In 2002, Yao moved to the United States. Now he plays professional basketball for the Houston Rockets. Yao and his mother live in a four-bedroom house in Houston. Yao's mother cooks Chinese food for him. He's learning English, and he's learning to drive a car.

Now look at the answers and write questions.

1. A: _____? **B:** On September 12, 1980.

2. A: _____? **B:** In Shanghai, China.

3. A: _____? **B:** At the Youth Sports School.

4. A: _____? **B:** In 2002.

2 **For each academic subject, write the occupation.**

1. architecture: _____

2. nursing: _____

3. science: _____

4. education: _____

5. engineering: _____

6. medicine: _____

7. law: _____

3 Get to know a famous person's life story. Choose a famous person. Answer the questions. Use the Internet, books, and other information.

1. Person's name: _____

2. When was he / she born? _____.

3. Where was he / she born? _____.

4. Where did he / she grow up? _____.

5. Where did he / she go to school? _____.

6. What did he / she study? _____.

7. Did he / she graduate? When? _____.

8. What does he / she do now? _____.

LESSON 2

4 What would you like to do in your life? Write four sentences. Look at the pictures and the verbs in the box for ideas.

 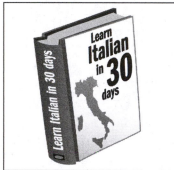 

move	have children	meet
study	go	see
graduate	learn	buy
get married		

Example: *I would like to go to Australia* _____.

1. _____.

2. _____.

3. _____.

4. _____.

5 ▷ Write <u>your</u> responses to good news and bad news.

1. "I'm going to graduate this year."

   (YOU) _____ .

2. "My parents are going to get divorced."

   (YOU) _____ .

3. "My grandfather died two days ago."

   (YOU) _____ .

4. "My wife and I are going to have a baby."

   (YOU) _____ .

5. "I met a nice, good-looking man. We're going to get married."

   (YOU) _____ .

6. "I'm going to move to London for work. I don't want to go."

   (YOU) _____ .

LESSON 3

6 ▷ What are you going to do this summer? Check ✔ the boxes.

☐ travel	☐ relax	☐ exercise
☐ go camping	☐ sleep late	☐ work
☐ go fishing	☐ do nothing	☐ go to school
☐ go bike riding	☐ hang out with friends	☐ move
☐ go to the beach	☐ go for walks	☐ get married

Now write to a friend about <u>your</u> plans. Write sentences with <u>be going to</u>.

7 Complete the conditional sentences, using **be going to**. Use real information.

1. If the weather is nice this weekend, _____.

2. If the weather isn't nice this weekend, _____.

3. If I have enough time this week, _____.

4. If I stay home tomorrow night, _____.

5. If I have enough money next year, _____.

8 Complete the conditional sentences. Use the present tense or **be going to**.

1. If it's warm tomorrow, I _____ to work.
   walk

2. If Matt _____, he's going to do poorly in this class.
   not study

3. We're going to buy shoes if we _____ to the mall.
   go

4. If Pamela takes a vacation this year, she _____.
   travel

5. They _____ a big family if they get married.
   have

6. Mr. and Mrs. Johnson are going to go out for dinner after the movie if it

   _____ too late.
   not be

9 A reporter from your school newspaper wants to write an article about you. Answer her questions about yourself.

1. When were you born?

_____

_____

2. Where were you born?

_____

_____

3. Where did you grow up?

_____

_____

4. What do you do?

_____

_____

5. What are you studying now?

_____

_____

6. What do you like to do in your free time?

_____

_____

7. What would you like to do in the next five years?

_____

_____

CLARION UNIVERSITY

JUST FOR FUN

 A RIDDLE FOR YOU!

When asked how old she was, Suzie answered, "In two years I'm going to be twice as old as I was five years ago." How old is she now?

a. Twelve.　　　　**b.** Seven.　　　　**c.** Fourteen.

2 **Complete the puzzle.**

Across

2. Go places

5. Academic subject for teachers

8. Go to live in a new home: ____

10. A very young person

11. Become husband and wife: ____ ____

12. Complete school

Down

1. A response to good news

3. The name of Heyerdahl's raft

4. Academic subject for doctors

6. Architecture, psychology, and law are all ____ ____.

7. A response to bad news: ____ ____

9. Take a nap

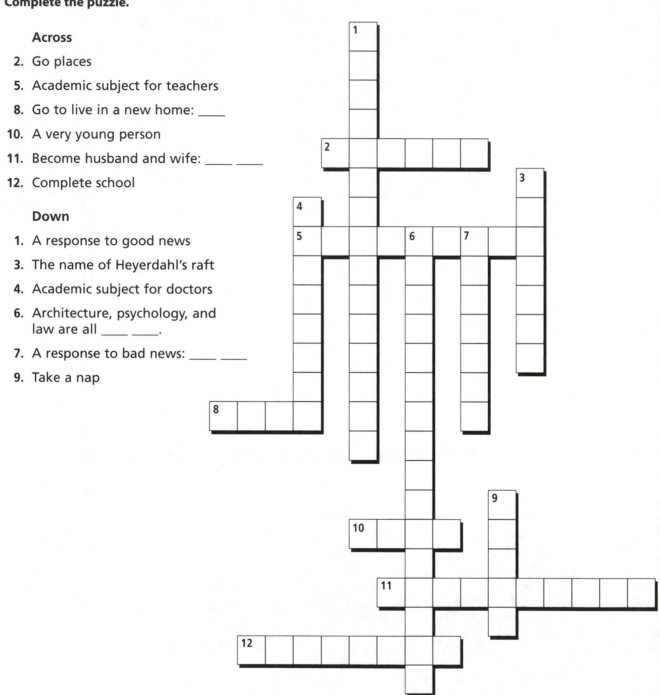

SOURCE: Created with Discovery's Puzzlemaker.

Riddle: a

88 UNIT 14

CHECKPOINT

1 ▶ **WHAT ABOUT YOU?** **Answer the questions.**

1. How often should you brush your teeth?

   _____.

2. Can you check e-mail on your cell phone?

   _____.

3. Are you listening to music right now?

   _____.

4. Can you cook fish well?

   _____.

5. Are you going to go running if the weather is nice this weekend?

   _____.

6. Would you like to go to the beach this summer?

   _____.

7. Where did you go on your last vacation?

   _____.

8. Where would you like to go on your next vacation?

   _____.

9. What can't you do? Would you like to learn?

   _____.

10. What should you study if you want to make a lot of money?

   _____.

2 ▶ **WEATHER REPORTS.** **Check** ✔ **yesterday's weather.**

☐ cloudy ☐ sunny ☐ windy ☐ cold
☐ hot ☐ warm ☐ cool

Now write sentences.

1. What was the weather like yesterday?

   _____.

2. What's the weather like today? Is it raining or snowing?

   _____.

3 **Read about Andrea Bocelli.**

He's an Italian opera singer, but people of all ages, young and old, listen to his music. He sings beautifully and is famous all over the world. He has dark, wavy hair and a beard. His name is Andrea Bocelli.

Bocelli was born on September 22, 1958 in Tuscany. He grew up on his family's farm. He started singing for family members when he was about three years old. When he was six, he

learned to play the piano. He can also play the flute and the saxophone. At the age of twelve, he had a soccer accident, and now he can't see. Bocelli graduated from the University of Pisa. He studied law, but he only worked for one year as a lawyer.

He started to study music. His teacher was the famous singer Franco Corelli. In the evenings, he sang in piano bars. During this time, he got married. He and his wife, Enrica, have two children, Amos and Matteo. In 1992, Luciano Pavarotti listened to a tape of Bocelli singing. This was good news for Bocelli's music career. Between 1994 and 2003, he made about 20 albums.

Bocelli lives in Monte Carlo. In the summer, he and his family live in Tuscany, where he grew up. Bocelli has a busy schedule. He studies music and practices singing for two hours or more every day. He travels a lot. He writes, too. He wrote a book about his life story, *The Music of Silence*. In his free time, he reads and cooks Italian food.

4 **To write this article, a reporter interviewed Andrea Bocelli. Answer the reporter's questions for Bocelli.**

1. **Reporter:** Where were you born?

   Bocelli: *I was born in Tuscany* _____.

2. **Reporter:** And did you grow up there?

   Bocelli: _____.

3. **Reporter:** What did you study?

   Bocelli: _____.

4. **Reporter:** Can you play any musical instruments?

   Bocelli: _____.

5. **Reporter:** When did you learn to play the piano?

   Bocelli: _____.

6. **Reporter:** Tell me about your family.

   Bocelli: _____.

7. **Reporter:** Where do you live now?

   Bocelli: _____.

8. **Reporter:** What is your daily schedule like?

   Bocelli: _____.

5 Look again at the article in Exercise 3. Circle all 19 simple past tense verbs in the article. Write 10 of these verbs on the lines. Then write the base form of the 10 verbs.

1. _was_ ➔ _be_   6. _____ ➔ _____
2. _____ ➔ _____   7. _____ ➔ _____
3. _____ ➔ _____   8. _____ ➔ _____
4. _____ ➔ _____   9. _____ ➔ _____
5. _____ ➔ _____   10. _____ ➔ _____

OPTIONAL VOCABULARY BOOSTER ACTIVITIES

1 Check ✔ the weather where you live. Then write the season(s).

| In what season(s)? |

1. ☐ thunderstorms   _____
2. ☐ snowstorms   _____
3. ☐ hurricanes   _____
4. ☐ tornadoes   _____

2 Make a fruit or vegetable salad. Write the ingredients on the recipe card.

_____ **Salad**

Ingredients:

3 Check ✔ the activities you do. Then circle your three favorite activities.

☐ go rock climbing   ☐ get a manicure
☐ go rollerblading   ☐ go ice skating
☐ play golf   ☐ go sailing
☐ go snorkeling   ☐ go horseback riding

How often do you do your three favorite activities?

1. _____.
2. _____.
3. _____.

4 **Circle the word or phrase that is different.**

1. grapefruit	(peach)	lemon	tangerine
2. dust	play	mop the floor	vacuum the house
3. go sailing	go snorkeling	go windsurfing	go rock climbing
4. knuckle	knee	calf	thigh
5. saxophone	flute	trumpet	drums
6. biology	drama	medicine	chemistry

5 **You're going to go to a beach resort for five days. All activities are included.**
Look at the activities you can do.

Do you want to be busy every minute or just relax on the beach? Look at all our great activities and make your plans.

And don't worry about the weather. It's always beautiful. Have a wonderful vacation!

play volleyball on the beach
play golf
go bike riding
go horseback riding
go swimming
go snorkeling
go sailing

go windsurfing
go fishing
go on a boat ride
go water skiing
exercise
get a manicure
go shopping

take a taxi to a nearby town
have dinner on your balcony
go on a dinner cruise
go for a walk on the beach
go dancing
take a nap or sleep late
relax or do nothing!

Complete the chart. Plan your morning, afternoon, and evening activities for each day.

	Morning	Afternoon	Evening
Saturday			
Sunday			
Monday			
Tuesday			
Wednesday			

Now answer these questions about your plans.

1. What are you going to do on Saturday morning? _____

2. What are you going to do on Tuesday afternoon? _____

3. What are you doing on Wednesday evening? _____

4. Are you going to go snorkeling? When? _____

5. Are you going to go windsurfing? When? _____

92 *Units 8–14*